Bubbles

Bubbles

A Self Portrait

by

BEVERLY SILLS

BOBBS-MERRILL

Indianapolis/New York

To Mama, Papa, Peter,
Muffy and Bucky

Acknowledgments

This book would not have been possible without the superb editorial assistance with both text and pictures of Milton Orshefsky.

My husband Peter was consistently helpful and jogged my memory on most of the events.

James G. Burke was responsible for much of the picture research.

Contents

Bubbles

1

"That's no seven-year-old! She's a midget"

Me at three, "The Most Beautiful Baby of 1932"—in Brooklyn.

When I was only three, and still named Belle Miriam Silverman, I sang my first aria in public. The stage was Tompkins Park, in Brooklyn, New York; the occasion, a contest to proclaim "Miss Beautiful Baby of 1932." I wore an outfit with a deep *décolleté* and I had no doubt I would win the title for Body. My song was a catchy little number entitled "The Wedding of Jack and Jill"; it won me the award for Talent, too. When the master of ceremonies for the event asked me my name, I replied, "Chewpee Bow Sipperman," which was as close as I could get to Cutie Pie Silverman, a pet name my father called me. That is, when he, my mother and my two brothers were not calling me "Bubbles," an endearment forced on me at birth because I was born with an enormous bubble of spit in my mouth. "That's an omen," the doctor said. "We *have* to call her 'Bubbles.'" The name has stuck.

I wish I could say that Tompkins Park was the start of my career. It wasn't, of course; there were no plans then for me to have a career. But my mother had, and still has, an intense passion for music and she passed it on to me. Among her collection of phonograph records were eleven old Madame Galli-Curci records—seventy-eights. She would play them even before she made coffee in the morning, and they would echo throughout the house all day long. Before I was seven, I had memorized all twenty-two arias on the recordings, and could sing them in phonetic Italian. My mother felt strongly that all little girls, whether they go on to college or not, should learn to sing, to tap dance, and to play the piano. Every Saturday morning I was schlepped downtown to a school and there, for a dollar, I was given singing lessons, dancing lessons, and elocution lessons. The last curriculum I did not really need; I was then, as I am now, a compulsive talker. I probably taught the elocution teacher a thing or two.

The school had a weekly Saturday morning local radio program on Station WOR called "Uncle Bob's Rainbow Hour," on which the more talented little pupils would get to perform. At four, I was not a sensational singer, piano player, or tap dancer but I did have a precocious tongue and vocabulary. They got me on the show. I would say some funny things with Uncle Bob Emory on the air and then he would allow me to sing. My big aria was still "The Wedding of Jack and Jill," which ended with the words "ding, dong, ding." Once, the live audience applauded before I finished the song, drowning out the ending. "Wait a minute!" I shrieked over the air waves. "I haven't finished my ding-dong!" That plaint became a kind of password with Uncle Bob and me; we still giggle over it.

Just before one of my scheduled appearances on the radio show, I was told by our doctor that I might be coming down with mumps, but I insisted on being taken to the studio for my regular "do" with Uncle Bob. On the air he said to me, "How do you feel today?" hoping to start a nice, funny conversation. "Not so good," I replied. "I have the mumps." Every male in the studio raced out in panic—except for Uncle Bob, who was saddled with me and the mike. He allowed me to finish my song and then I was taken home. I did, it turned out, have the mumps.

Uncle Bob gave his kids, including me, maximum public exposure. Once he rented Town Hall to present the talent and I got to sing a coloratura aria that I had picked up from Galli-Curci's records—"*Il Bacio*." My performance moved one New York columnist to accuse Uncle Bob, half-seriously, of misrepresentation. "That's no seven-year-old!" the columnist wrote. "She's a midget."

When I was seven, and renamed Beverly Sills (a friend of my mother's thought that some day it might look better on a marquee than Belle Silverman), Twentieth Century-Fox made one attempt to make a movie star out of me. In American cultural history we were at the beginning of the *Wunderkind* era. Shirley Temple was at her peak, Bobby Breen was making it big with Eddie Cantor, and Deanna Durbin and Judy Garland were about to check in. I, meanwhile, had been heard singing my Italian arias in the Queen Mary Restaurant in New York City by a studio director and asked to sing something in an educational-type film called *Uncle Sol Solves It*, starring Willy Howard.

I sang in the movie but I did not conquer Hollywood. My mother wasn't a stage mother pushing, pushing me into a career and at that point I still had no formal voice training—I was simply singing imitations of Galli-Curci. But the experience at least made my parents think that perhaps there *was* something to this little girl who was singing all those arias at such an early age. My mother decided that the time had come to have someone listen to me who could make an honest evaluation of my talent.

One day, as we were walking along Fifty-seventh Street, in Manhattan, we noticed on a newsstand near Carnegie Hall a magazine called "Musical Courier." On its cover was a picture of Estelle Liebling captioned "Coach to the World's Greatest Voices." My mother had already determined that if I was going to be anything, it would have to be the greatest; she called Miss Liebling and made an appointment. When we arrived at her studio, Miss Liebling took one look at this beautiful lady, my mother, and said to her: "Leave the little girl with the secretary. I'll hear you sing right now." "Oh, no, no," my mother said. "The audition is for my little girl." "But I don't teach children," Miss Liebling replied. Then, after a pause, "In fact, I don't even *know* any children."

That could have been the end of Beverly Sills right there. But when my mother explained that we had come all the way from Sea Gate—which is past Coney Island—and that we had been traveling for an hour and a half on one bus, one trolley, and two subway trains, Miss Liebling agreed to listen to me. Heretofore, every time I had done my little vocal routine for adults they had gone crazy with applause. Now, when I finished singing my *"Il Bacio"* for Miss Liebling, she burst out laughing. *I* burst out crying: *nobody* had ever laughed at me before. Much later she explained to me what had set off her laughter. My Italian, learned phonetically from old records of dubious quality, came out so funny that it was nonexistent. At the same time she was bowled over by the idea of a seven-year-old imitating the famous Galli-Curci trill.

In any event, Miss Liebling must have been impressed: she agreed to teach me one day a week for fifteen minutes. That, she said, would be quite long enough for my still-fragile young voice. Every Saturday my mother and I would travel three hours portal-to-portal so that I could sing fifteen minutes of scales. It must have been quite a chore for Miss Liebling, too. Like all seven-year-olds, I was extremely wiggly. I had to stand in the middle of a big circular pattern in the Oriental rug in her studio and try not to fidget while singing for fifteen minutes. It wasn't easy.

Miss Liebling was an incredible teacher. She had been an opera singer, making her debut in *Lucia di Lammermoor* with the Dresden Royal Opera Company. She had studied with Mathilde Marchesi, one of the great voice teachers of all time. Madame Marchesi had numbered among her pupils Emma Calvé, Emma Eames, Mary Garden, and Nellie Melba. Miss Liebling taught the Marchesi method; when she died in 1970 she was, I think, the last surviving pupil of Mme. Marchesi. Her own pupils had included Galli-Curci, Frieda Hempel, and Maria Jeritza. She had a marvelous technique: even in her eighties she could occasionally sing beautiful tones. She is the only singing teacher I have ever had on a continuing basis. Our association started in 1936 and lasted until her death—thirty-four years!

Miss Liebling was more than a teacher to me, she was a second mother;

and as she was older than my real mother, she was even more matriarchal. I was married in her studio. When she died, at ninety-two, she left me in her will a beautiful Sèvres china cup. It was the same cup in which she would have hot chocolate waiting for me when I showed up in her studio in the middle of winter, freezing from that long commute from Sea Gate. I have never been more touched.

After my first two years with Miss Liebling she decided it was time to display my new, polished singing voice to the public. She was a good friend of Major Bowes, who at that time had a very successful weekly radio program on CBS called "Major Bowes' Amateur Hour," and she set up an audition for me. I was accepted, appeared on the show singing *"Caro Nome"* from *Rigoletto*, another aria I had learned from a Galli-Curci record, and I won the amateur contest. As a result, I became a regular member of Major Bowes' Capitol Family Hour show, which broadcast nation-wide every Sunday from the old Capitol Theater Building in New York City.

The Major and I got along famously. On the air we would chat, as I had done with Uncle Bob. I was less funny now but I used more and bigger words. Then I would sing. What I didn't realize at first was what an enormous audience the program had; it went into millions of homes. The first time I appeared on the Capitol Family Hour Major Bowes gave me a tiny glass elephant. When he announced over the air that I was clutching the elephant for good luck when I performed, I began receiving in the mail hundreds of elephants—to supplement the lovely jade and ivory ones the Major kept giving me. I eventually wound up with a huge collection of elephants. Once on his program I made the mistake of saying on the air that I would love to have a sled because it was snowing outside; I received twenty-five sleds from listeners, all of which we distributed to various orphanages and schools except one, an all-chrome job from the Kalamazoo Sled Company, which I was allowed to keep. And when I told on the program how my mother made all my clothes for me and how I was hoping, now that I was ten, that she would allow me to wear a long dress, dozens of long dresses streamed at me through the mails. It was wonderful.

My father took a rather dim view of theatrical children, but he went along with my extracurricular activities because he believed enthusiastically in education in any form and I was certainly getting that. In addition to my singing lessons, I was studying piano—at Miss Liebling's insistence—with Paolo Gallico, father of the writer Paul Gallico. He was a great teacher— and a hard taskmaster: I had ten red knuckles at the end of every lesson because he would bang a ruler across my knuckles if I had not practiced enough or done as well as he felt I should. It was affectionately done—I think. He gave me books to read and introduced me to all kinds of interesting literature about famous pianists. I was also, at my father's insistence, learning foreign languages. I already spoke French because shortly after I was born a French maid had come to live with us. There we were, my brothers and I—three little kids from Brooklyn running around the house talking French! By the time I was ten I could speak Italian too, and I had already learned *Rigoletto.* Gilda was the first role Miss Liebling taught me.

It was all fun. Public school on weekdays, then to Manhattan on Saturday for piano lessons, language lessons, singing lessons, lunch with my mother at a Horn and Hardart Cafeteria, the Roxy Theatre to take in a movie, to Chinatown for supper with the whole family, and then back to Brooklyn. Sundays I would be taken to my regular stint with the Major. My original twenty-two Galli-Curci arias had expanded into some fascinating new repertoire and I was enjoying every minute of it.

Through Major Bowes' Capitol Family Hour came an offer to me to appear in a soap opera called "Our Gal Sunday." I signed on for thirty-six weeks, at $67.50 per fifteen-minute broadcast, playing the role of Elaine Raleigh, a little mountain girl whose drunken father continually abuses her, forcing her to take refuge in song and in the hills. One guest star was Esther Ralston of silent screen fame; she played a famous opera singer from New York who happens to visit, hears this young mountain gal singing in the hills, and takes her back to the city—never to be heard of again.

Probably a good thing, too, because I had just turned twelve and my parents decided that I was ready for retirement and a more normal existence.

To tell the truth, I was ready for retirement myself. I was beginning to look a little awkward. I had already done a number of exciting things— soap opera, Major Bowes, a Rinso White commercial. I had been one of the first children ever to be telecast on NBC for a program called "Stars of the Future." Then, too, Major Bowes had become seriously ill and the Capitol Family had been replaced on the air with a program called "The Cresta Blanca Carnival," a program of music played by the Morton Gould orchestra. Now instead of my regular talking-and-singing visits with Major Bowes, I was a soloist with Gould, along with a young man who had, and still has, one of the most beautiful baritone voices I have ever heard. He was then called Merill Miller; his name is now Robert Merrill.

Even in retirement I was to continue all my lessons, going to the City by myself every Saturday on subways, then judged safe, with four dollars pinned inside my bloomers for the various lessons and two nickels in my pocket for all the transportation. The rest of the week I was an ordinary Brooklyn teenager. We lived in an all-Jewish neighborhood in a house much like all the others in that Sea Gate area—two stories, detached, six rooms (three of them bedrooms on the second floor), and a little Victory Garden at the back. Our front yard was the Atlantic Ocean. I had a "steady," a boy named Sandy Levine, aged fifteen, who used to drive my father out of his mind. Sandy would never come into our house to fetch me; instead he would hang around outside all day long, and when he wanted to summon me he would whistle the tune of my Rinso White commercial—"Rinso White, Rinso White, happy little washday song." "Are you going out," my father used to ask me, "with a boy or a bird?"

I was attending P.S. 91, an elementary school in Brooklyn, and was an associate editor of the school newspaper, the *Herald*. When I was graduated in 1942, the paper published its annual Personality Poll. I was voted Prettiest Girl, Most Likely to Succeed, Fashion Plate, Most Talented, and Most Personality. I was *not* voted Smartest or Wittiest or—surprise!—Most Talkative.

The dream at that early age of my eventually becoming an opera star was mine, not my mother's. But it was she who made me believe that the impossible dream was possible. In her eyes, anything that her three children wanted to be, they could be—and she would support them all the way. Even though my father's attitude at the time was that there was no place in *his* family for a theatrical child, he continued to rationalize his reluctant approval of what my mother and I were doing: at least I was getting a good musical education. I was already a good enough pianist for Mr. Gallico to urge my mother to allow me to concentrate solely on the piano. And my father loved the fact that I was becoming multilingual; the idea of my eventually sitting at a dinner party conversing in several languages would have appealed to him. That is probably what was in the back of his mind— not the idea that, oh goody, she'll be able to sing opera in three different languages. At that time my mother never really considered the possibility of my becoming a famous opera singer either. I think that what delighted her most, given her own passion for music, was that what delighted *me* most was singing.

They were happy times, and to me, at least, quite normal. I never thought that I was doing anything special. I was doing something I loved with the backing of both my parents—though admittedly for different reasons, with different goals in mind.

Bubbles at five months.

The Silverman kids—
Sydney, eight, Bubbles, three, Stanley, six.

Papa—in his mid-forties.

At P.S. 232 in Brooklyn in 1935,
our first grade put on a play called
Sur le Pont d'Avignon. *The boy*
is Albert Silverstein. *Forty-one*
years later we bumped into each other
on Beverly Sills Day in Brooklyn.

20

The show must go on. It did, at Uncle Bob's Rainbow House program in 1936—although the studio was evacuated in panic except for Uncle Bob and me when I broke the dreaded news: I had MUMPS.

My professional pose at age ten. Note how little it has changed since that Tompkins Park contest.

Celebrating with Major Bowes on his Capitol Family Hour in 1939.

2

Thank God
Pons had a light, high voice!

Lily Pons in Lakmé.

My mother took me to see my first opera when I was eight years old. It was Delibes' *Lakmé* at the Metropolitan, with Lily Pons in the title role. Miss Pons, a little Dresden doll, came on stage in a costume that had a brief halter top and a lot of bare midriff. It was, for those days, an extremely *risqué* outfit. I got so excited that I yelled at the top of my lungs, "Mama, Mama, her belly button is showing!"

I was hooked. I became an instant Pons fan, so overwhelmed by her performance that I wrote her a letter about how beautiful she was and how beautifully she sang. She wrote back inviting Mama and me to a concert she was giving at Carnegie Hall. I began to collect her recordings—*The Daughter of the Regiment, Rigoletto*—and I fell in love with the bell-like quality of her voice. Not only was her voice remarkable; she also *looked* all her roles. That was not the case then for most opera stars; it was still the era of the singer, not the singer-actress. Lily looked so much like Lakmé, so much like Gilda, so much like the little girl in *The Daughter of the Regiment* that I began to get interested in the actual stories of operas and the characters in them. I asked my mother to buy me a book of opera stories, and that Christmas I was given a large yellow volume entitled *Operas Every Child Should Know*. It was a Bible for me; there is no other book that I have reread as often.

When I studied my first role, Gilda, with Miss Liebling, she made me translate the entire opera from Italian into English in my own words, without using the libretto. The idea, of course, in addition to helping my Italian, was to teach me what the story meant in my own terms. (I had no idea at that young age, for example, that Gilda was abducted and raped by the Count, and I kept asking Miss Liebling, "What's she so excited about? What's the big deal? Here she is in this beautiful castle and she's got this handsome Duke . . ." I thought it was all pretty terrific!)

I credit Pons, in a way, for getting me interested in characterization on stage, which later became an integral part of my singing. I realize now that often she looked the part more than she actually portrayed it. In *Lucia*, for example, her performance was much more vocal than dramatic. During the Mad Scene she wore a beautiful white satin nightgown with a red velvet stole that made a kind of slash across her costume. She was very stage-wise and costume-wise, yet she barely moved during the scene. To me, though, she looked like Lucia, she *was* Lucia.

Although I was in forced withdrawal from public performing, I attended a good many musical functions. Miss Liebling was always giving me tickets to operas, and she opened a whole new world to me. She used to invite my mother and me to dinner at her home. We would sit at table surrounded by famous singers—Maria Jeritza, Jessica Dragonette, Grace Moore, Lauritz Melchior, Lucy Monroe, and many others—and after dinner I would be asked by Miss Liebling to sing a little song or two for the evening's entertainment. Miss Liebling knew that I loved soufflés, and whenever I came to dinner the dessert was chocolate soufflé or one of the courses was cheese soufflé. Della, the cook, would say, "I knew you were invited tonight because Miss Liebling told me to make lots of soufflés."

At her parties Miss Liebling would stand up and deliver funny speeches. I was always amazed that she was so much at ease on her feet, and I think that I have unconsciously copied her style, because I feel very free and easy now when I talk in front of large groups. She taught me to talk to people as though on a one-to-one basis, and she had a kind of funny twinkle in her eye, so that even when she was saying something that was rather unpleasant it was said in good humor.

For a girl in her early teens those glamorous evenings at Miss Liebling's were heady drink. They gave me a taste of a kind of life I thought might be great fun—the life of an opera star. Miss Liebling may even have had the Metropolitan Opera in mind for me; she often told me of her excitement when she performed at the Berlin Opera, and of how she used to tour all over the United States giving more than a thousand concerts with John Phillip Sousa. So far, *my* longest traveling had been from Brooklyn to Manhattan plus an occasional journey to New Jersey for summer camp. I was dreaming of travel, of long train rides, and the kinds of experiences I was hearing about only made me want more and more to be a singer.

Over those years I built up a large repertoire; by the time I was fifteen, I knew twenty operas. Miss Liebling was extremely shrewd in her choice of repertoire for me—she kept it very light and very high. She had published books of ornamentation for the coloratura voice, and as I was still learning to sing by imitation, she would sing for me and I would try to duplicate the sound. She had a fantastic trill; I learned to trill simply by listening to her and imitating her. The main thing that Miss Liebling gave me was a solid technique. She stressed breath control and my whole technique of singing is based on it. As a result, I know how to sing. Even when I have laryngitis and cannot speak, I am almost always able to sing.

By then I was traveling from Brooklyn to Miss Liebling's studio in the city three or four times a week and my lessons had expanded to 45 minutes or an hour, depending upon what we wanted to accomplish. (I could never have afforded her usual fee—about $25 per hour. Although my father was an assistant manager in a Metropolitan Life Insurance office and we were not poor, we were more in the $2 per hour bracket than the $25. But Miss Liebling refused to take a penny for any of my lessons in all the years I was with her, even when I was able to afford it. By that time I was a member of her family, she of mine, and the question of money was naturally never broached.) She piled music on me and I absorbed it like a sponge. Everything in the *bel canto* repertoire delighted me. Primarily because of my worship of Lily Pons, I wanted to sing everything she sang—*The Daughter of the Regiment, Rigoletto*, Rosina in *The Barber of Seville*. Thank God Pons had a light, high voice! Heaven help me if I had worshiped Kirsten Flagstad instead. But even that would not have stopped me; I would have memorized Flagstad's repertoire too, because I was just plain nuts about opera. I have even memorized about ten operas that I never want to sing and never will sing. I learned them because I loved them. When, for example, I saw the debut of Ljuba Welitch in *Salomé* at the Met in 1949, I became a Strauss buff. I learned Salomé but I don't want to sing her. I've learned Elektra too, but I will never be able to sing her—it requires a totally different voice from mine.

In 1944, when I was fifteen, I decided to come out of retirement. I began reading theatrical publications for announcements of chorus auditions for Broadway musicals. You must understand that for a fifteen-year-old-girl who dreamed of being an opera star, the starting possibilities then were nil. The New York City Opera had not yet been established. There were fewer opera companies than there are today, and no regional companies. Miss Liebling thought it was a good idea for me to begin auditioning around because it would give me opportunities to sing before live audiences. (I had sung before large numbers of people only a few times in my life—on Major Bowes' Amateur Hour; at an amateur contest in junior high school, where I won ten dollars and a policeman had to escort me and my enormous earnings home; at the première of my movie at the Savoy Theatre in Brooklyn when I was seven, attended by about half the Metropolitan Life Insurance Company; and at Miss Liebling's dinner parties for twenty-five people.) But she did not like the idea of my auditioning for Broadway choruses; *no* self-respecting would-be opera star, she felt, should take a job as a chorus singer, much less in a chorus line.

Nevertheless, I went auditioning. I had turned into a tall, statuesque fifteen-year-old with very long blond hair. I must have looked like a show girl because I was offered every chorus job I ever auditioned for. I turned them all down. But at one chorus audition for a Broadway show that J. J. Shubert was producing—it was called *Love in the Snow*—I was offered the job of understudy to Anne Jeffreys, the star. When I raced home to break the news, my father, who was not aware that I had been auditioning, hit the ceiling. Out of the question, he said. I was going to get a college education first, and *then* if I wanted to go on stage, fine. But I was going to have a college degree in my pocket in case things didn't work out for me on the stage.

That was that. In our house, as in most Jewish middle-class households of the time, the father's word was law. And my father was a very positive man; every sentence he spoke had a period at the end. When I was about thirteen, for example, he said to me, "Listen, your mother doesn't smoke and she doesn't drink and you're not going to either and that's the end of the discussion." And it was. I never smoked and I still do not drink, except wine. There was never a question of my rebelling against my father's decision about the Shubert offer, or of running away from home. Besides, I loved my father.

Once more unto the breach, dear Miss Liebling. She knew J. J. Shubert well and arranged for me to have an audition with the great man himself. It was love at first sight. I guess that I was the baby girl J. J. had never had and perhaps he was the grandpa I had never had. We read scripts together, both of us playing all kinds of parts and he trying hard to get rid of my Brooklyn accent. He brought people in to teach me how to wear makeup. Frequently we would have dinner in his apartment and do jigsaw puzzles. Then I would subway back to Brooklyn, doing my homework on board, so that I would be home—as agreed—by nine o'clock.

I was enjoying myself tremendously—making new friends, exploring

Greenwich Village (whose life style then was considerably different from what it is now). I discovered the art film, mostly French, and was suddenly aware that there was a Europe on the other side of the ocean. Would I ever get to France, I dreamed, where everyone must look like Lily Pons?

I remember standing room at the Met, holding an armful of school books, wearing bobby socks and brown-and-white saddle shoes and a big Sloppy Joe sweater, listening to the opera and wanting it to go on forever. The war was on and we lived in terrible fear because both my brothers were in combat service. From Norton Point, the farthest tip of Sea Gate, we could see the ships being loaded with soldiers leaving for Europe and the wind would bring back the sounds of their voices—the saddest sound in the world.

It was a crazy-mixed-up time in my life—I was growing up. Musically it was an incredibly exhilarating period. What J. J. was cooking up for me was a Gilbert and Sullivan repertory tour that would enable me to sing roles in seven different operettas. But first there were my parents to convince. My father was dead against it—I was too young, he said, he didn't want my mother to travel with me, she belonged at his side, and so on. But J. J.—and my mother—finally won. Mama found a chaperone for me, a nice, religious girl in the cast. She was to room with me, see that my clothes were packed properly, that I made all the trains, was taken to the theater and brought straight home afterwards. And off we went on tour. My chaperone was also supposed to do my hair, using a recipe my mother had invented to keep it a lovely golden color. The recipe called for two parts of gold bleach to one part of red rinse, plus peroxide. The chaperone got it backwards—two parts red to one part gold. That's how I became a redhead. I liked it and I have remained a redhead ever since.

The only trouble with my chaperone was that she had a tendency to entertain her men friends in our room until the wee hours. When Mama learned of this, through a letter a chorus boy in the cast wrote her, she promptly fired the girl chaperone and appointed her informant my chaperone for the rest of the tour. (*That* chaperone later served a term in jail for murder. We corresponded all during his term and he sent me the most gorgeous needlepoint pillows he had made. A week after he was paroled, he died of a heart attack and my husband and I helped bury him.)

It was 1945 and I was sixteen. My salary was $100 a week—which seemed an enormous sum at the time—out of which my father insisted that I buy a twenty-five-dollar war bond. By that time I had transferred from Erasmus High School in Brooklyn to the Professional Children's School in Manhattan. While on tour I finished that school's curriculum via a correspondence course. My father couldn't bear the idea of my graduating with a correspondence-course diploma; to him it was a waste of my brain. He was even more upset when Frank Fay, who handed out the diplomas at graduation, patted me on the fanny as I went by and said, "Boy, they didn't make them like you when *I* was graduating!"

My father was very worried about my future. To show him that I was

still his smart little baby girl, I won a mathematics scholarship to Fairleigh Dickinson College. He was overjoyed and kept urging me to take advantage of the scholarship. But I had other ideas. I had returned from the Gilbert and Sullivan tour with a fistful of marvelous reviews. I had learned a good deal about stagecraft. I had learned how to project my speaking voice on stage. (Although my accent has always remained New York, I did at least manage to get rid of a good bit of the Brooklyn tinge. You just don't perform Gilbert and Sullivan sounding as though you came from the Ebbetts Field bleachers.) I had worked very hard with my music, I was a very disciplined young girl, and my desire to perform in front of an audience had become insatiable. Fairleigh Dickinson? Not a chance. I was going to be an opera star—and a very serious one. Period.

The Mikado, *as done by Camp Lincoln and Laurel in New Jersey in 1940. The star in the center is me, eleven, "Yum-Yum" Silverman, in a costume made by my mother. The handsome boy on my left is Buddy Israel, playing Nanki-Poo. Buddy went on to become Jules Irving, formerly director of the Vivian Beaumont Theatre in Lincoln Center and now a Hollywood TV producer. Buddy gave me my first kisses—offstage and on, both memorable.*

29

Graduation from P.S. 91. I was twelve. I made the dress myself—the first and last sewing I ever did. My brother Stanley took the picture and gave it to me as a graduation present; maybe he should have destroyed the negative.

Below, left, J.J. Shubert, the theatrical producer who launched my career by sending me on a Gilbert and Sullivan tour in 1945. At right, on that tour, that's my fifteen-year-old, grown-up-woman smile.

Miss Estelle Liebling, for thirty-four years my one and only voice teacher, in a portrait done in 1939.

3

"No, Morris, this one will be an opera singer"

And then, suddenly, I'm nineteen.

In 1946, when I was seventeen, J. J. Shubert bought me my first pair of high-heeled shoes and sent me out on tour again. This time out we were a repertory company of three shows. My two were *The Merry Widow* and *Countess Maritza*; a lady named Blanche Chanson—which I thought was the best stage name in the whole world—did *Rose Marie*. With my first high heels, my first strapless gown, and my first upswept hairdo, I didn't know what to hold up first on stage—the gown, the feet, or the hairdo. My very handsome leading man was Frank Melton. My salary was $150 per week and I was saving $37.50 of it in savings bonds, per my father's new instructions. I was billed as "The Youngest Primadonna in Captivity."

Playing The Merry Widow was fun (through the years I was to do the role several hundred times). In Gilbert and Sullivan I could always simply play myself; in *Patience*, for example, I played myself with a crisper accent. *The Merry Widow* was the first time I had to take on somebody else as a character and I loved it.

Even though I had no part, even as understudy, in *Rose Marie*, I used to watch every performance. One night I walked into the theater to find pandemonium backstage: a ballet dancer who played the part of Wanda, the Indian girl, had ptomaine poisoning. Would I do the part? Would I! At the moment my hair was very curly, set for the next day's matinée of *The Merry Widow*, and the makeup crew had only fifteen minutes to try to braid it so that I would look a little more like an Indian girl. Somebody raced next door to the grocery store and came back with six milk bottles, whose wire caps were then roughly fashioned into six stays to try to turn my hair into flat pigtails. Fat chance—by the time I got to the famous Indian Totem Tom-Tom Dance my pigtails were curled in great hooks at each end. My favorite line in the operetta was, "You come to my cabin later, huh?" Still all-absorbed in the Widow, I made it: "You come to my *castle* later, huh?"

The Shubert tour was invaluable experience for me, and the love Mr. Shubert bestowed on me is something I shall never forget. I had been around long enough to know what the name Shubert meant in the world of the theater and here was J. J. grooming *me* to be a star of the musical theater. It was somewhat off my original dream of being an opera star, but at the time it seemed the logical road to my eventual destination.

My parents, however, saw it differently and threw a roadblock. I remember a conversation the family had had during dinner one night when I was fourteen. I had been urging my mother to please tell Papa that I wanted to be an opera star and that he really ought to have a more positive attitude about it. As she served him his favorite dinner she said, "Listen, Morris, the child wants to be an opera star." He never looked up from the soup and replied, "The child will go to college and be smart." Mother: "No, Morris, the two boys will go to college and be smart. *This* one will be an opera singer."

My father was now reconciled to that dream of his two ladies, but he disagreed with my notion that through Broadway I would wind up in the opera. So did my mother. They told me firmly that I had to settle down, not spend three months on the road doing tours, without singing lessons, without piano lessons, without adding to my repertoire. That would get me nowhere. Either aim for a serious career, they ordered, or go back to school and become a music teacher.

And so my whole career with the Shuberts ended. To J. J.'s credit, he agreed with my parents' decision. He had felt when I first auditioned for him that for a young American artist eager to be an opera singer there was too little opportunity. Hordes of American singers, especially men who had just come back from the service, were returning to Europe to sing because there was no opportunity for them here. The Metropolitan was called an international house but the handful of Americans on its roster were treated like poor relations compared to the European singers. The whole country at the time was Europe-oriented as far as culture was concerned. If a singer's name was unpronounceable, why, of course, she was a great opera singer; if her name was pronounceable, how could she be great? We still had an inferiority complex toward the arts. J. J. was much more aware of that cultural syndrome than my family and I were at the time.

Reluctantly, I quit show biz and returned to serious study with Miss Liebling. By the time I was nineteen I had a repertoire of fifty or sixty operas. I was beginning to speak German. Not well—I have never been able to speak it well—but my accent is good and I can converse in it although not with the fluency of Italian or French. Miss Liebling was working hours with me on my repertoire, my style of singing, my coloratura technique. It was a period of intense training—and of very little employment.

But I did, finally, make my operatic debut. I played the role of Frasquita, one of Carmen's gypsy gang, in a Philadelphia Opera Company production in which Winifred Heidt and Eugene Conley, who were then married to each other, played Carmen and Don José. Guiseppe Bamboschek, the conductor, was a good friend of Miss Liebling's and he allowed me to understudy many roles with the company. I knew, because the Philadelphia was strictly star-oriented, that I would never be allowed to fill in even if a star singer did get sick, but at least I was able to watch great artists at work. I got to know Armando Annini, a fine stage director; he would tell me wonderful stories about Grace Moore, Jan Kiepura, Ezio Pinza, Lucrezia Bori, and about how Claudia Muzio would do the letter scene in *Traviata,* all of which further stirred my imagination and my desire to be an opera star.

Annini also taught me the Italian approach to stage acting. It was a kind of *verismo* approach, very much the style in those days—posy, blood-and-gutsy, featuring highly exaggerated makeup, especially for the eyes, and extensive overacting. When I saw my first *Thaïs,* done by the Philadelphia Company, I was struck by Florence Quatararo, a beautiful girl with a beautiful voice, who played the title role in a highly individualistic manner, not at all in the *verismo* style, and I realized that there must be another style of acting. Annini explained that the French school of acting was entirely different from the Italian. That is when my affinity for French opera began. I went through a passionately French period and in a very short time learned *Manon, Louise, Thaïs, Sapho, Faust,* and all the roles in *The Tales of Hoffman.* I just couldn't get enough of French repertoire.

In 1948, Miss Liebling, wanting to find some employment for her young singers, formed a group called the Estelle Liebling Singers. We were five girls and one baritone and we toured university and college towns. We had a good time, and each of us took home about $75 per concert, after expenses, but I was not getting any closer to being an opera star and I felt thoroughly frustrated.

In the latter part of the year my father had to undergo a series of operations. Only he and my mother knew how ill he was. He was in the hospital in August 1949 when I was offered a three-week tour to South America on a Moore-McCormack Line ship to do two concerts down and two back. My parents thought I should go and told me my father's condition was not serious. What they didn't tell me, of course, was that he was dying of lung cancer; he had been a four-packs-a-day man. My father, I think, preferred that I not see him physically deteriorate, and so, unknowing, I went off to

South America. The day I returned my mother met me at the pier, dressed in black: my father had died five days earlier.

Those were bleak times. At the beginning of my father's illness we had moved into Manhattan and taken a large apartment in the Stuyvesant Town complex, so that he could have treatments at Bellevue Hospital, which was nearby. When he died, my mother and I moved into a one-bedroom apartment in the same building and began what was a very lonely, close existence. My brothers were off at school—Sidney in medical school and Stanley at a teachers' college. My father had left us enough money to live on, although not in the same style as before. Life was manageable, but I was twenty years old, going nowhere, and very, very down.

One day, after my lesson with Miss Liebling, I was walking down Park Avenue looking into store windows. I must have been humming. Suddenly, next to my reflection in the window appeared that of a very distinguished-looking man in his sixties, wearing a derby and pince-nez. In a very clipped accent he asked me, "Are you a singer?" I said yes. He gave me his card; a member of a very prominent family in New York City, he ran an after-hours club open only to a very select membership and the club was looking for a woman who could sing and entertain the members. He hired me at $125 a week to sing at his club, which was on the East Side between Park and Madison. I would sing twenty minutes at a stretch and accompany myself on the piano, doing popular music as well as operatic if I liked, and then I would sit in a nearby lounge for forty minutes, reading a book. The hours were terrible, from ten P.M. to three A.M. but I was picked up in Stuyvesant Town and driven back every night. The first night I sang there I realized that this was not your average clientele; there were some of the biggest names in politics and business, names I had been reading in the newspaper. It was a private club with its own chef, where customers and clients could eat, drink, and be entertained without being seen by people they did not want to be seen by.

I was quite shocked one night, after having done my twenty minutes of song for a well-known name in the jewelry world, when the head waiter, who was very protective of me—always making sure that no one got too near me or said anything unpleasant—brought me back a hundred-dollar bill. "The gentleman you sang for," he said, "liked you very much and wants to give you a present." "I don't sing for tips," I said. My friend the head waiter replied, "Oh, yes, you do. Don't be ridiculous. You take that hundred dollars and enjoy it. You earn every penny you get." I took it.

Miss Liebling knew I had taken a job singing in a private club, but I never told her that the hours were ten to three. She felt that the best time to take a singing lesson was ten o'clock in the morning, and I could never persuade her to make it any later. The result was that I would stagger into bed at about four A.M. and stagger out again at nine to get to her studio on time. There were times when I was a bit groggy. My mother was not enthusiastic about my job, but she sensed my need to become somewhat independent and to feel that I was making a contribution to our existence. I think she also felt that my seeing that kind of after-hours life-style was in some way good for me: it certainly made me grow up quickly. Until then I had led a rather sheltered life within the bosom of my family. I had had boy friends, of course, but as the youngest child and the baby girl of the family, I was always extremely protected by my parents and my two brothers. My brothers believed, I think, as my mother did, that I would eventually become what I wanted to be, but during that growing-up time they treated me very much as the baby sister. We were inseparable as children. If one went to the movies, the three of us went. If Sidney wanted to see the Brooklyn Dodgers at Ebbetts Field, the three of us had to go. We always sat in the bleachers and to this day my mother is convinced that what cleared up my bad sinus condition as a child was the hours we spent under that baking Ebbetts Field sun. She may be right: whatever the reason, I did lose my sinus problems in the bleachers.

I continued to work at the after-hours club until I was twenty-one. By then I had made enough money to quit and take my mother to Europe. A fellow passenger on the ship, the *De Grasse*, was a lady named Gypsy Rose Lee. Aboard ship she and I would do benefit performances for the Seamen's Pension Fund. A lovely, bright, witty gal, she was a joy to be with. When the time came at those benefits to collect the money from the audience, she would say, "If you pay to hear Beverly sing, I'll let you stuff the dough down my bosom. She has her thing, I have mine."

Armed with a letter of introduction from Miss Liebling, I was accepted by Max de Rieux of the Paris Opéra into his acting class. There were eight singers, I the only American. Max taught me *Louise* and we went through *Manon* together. All the instruction was entirely in French and my accent improved tremendously; I was now as at home in French as in English. My mother and I had a marvelous time that summer. We stayed at a lovely small hotel, did the Louvre, the Lido, the Bateaux Mouches. We saw Paris the way I had always dreamed of seeing it and I had no desire to visit any other European city.

When we returned to New York at the end of summer, Miss Liebling was excited by the progress I had made and by my fascination with French repertoire. My mother was also very much involved in what I was doing. She still sewed all my clothes and did my hair, whipping up the ingredients with an eggbeater and brushing the result into my curls with a toothbrush. She is a remarkable lady and was a most unselfish mother—she always put her own life's desires second to those of her children. That's why, I think, she never married again. She was still a beautiful and talented woman and she certainly had lots of opportunities. But she always felt that as long as any of her children—in this case, me—was still at home and needed her she would not marry; she could never bring a strange man into the house while she had children living with her. Then by the time I had married she was so caught up in her grandmother role—my oldest brother had produced an heir and my other brother was married—that she apparently didn't feel the need to share her life with anyone other than the family she already had.

We still had some money and my spirits were high but I was once again in the familiar position of having no place to go. Regional operas were in their infancy and jobs were hard to find. The New York City Opera was going strong but I did not audition for them at the time. Why not is still a mystery to me. I suppose I felt, as a great many people still feel, that it is impossible to get into the New York City Opera. Actually, it is the easiest thing in the world to get an audition with them. In one way I'm happy that I didn't even try then—I had absolutely no experience in opera, simply a huge repertoire that nobody had ever heard me sing publicly.

Miss Liebling must have felt the same way: she never suggested that I try the City Opera. Instead she moved me into more repertoire. I was learning German songs. I went through books and books of Schubert *lieder*. She taught me the role of Sophie in *Der Rosenkavalier*, my first German role. She and my mother would always talk as though they were sure that some day, when the moment was absolutely right, everything good would begin happening to me. I was younger and more impatient. I knew that I was a rather attractive young woman. I felt somehow that *something* should begin to click soon. But nothing seemed to be happening and I did not want to return to the after-hours club. I wanted to get opera offers. I began to nag Miss Liebling to arrange an audition for me at the Metropolitan.

On tour in 1947 in The Merry Widow. *I'm the Widow in the center with my first strapless gown, my first upswept hairdo. Decorously holding hands with me is the leading man, Frank Melton.*

In her studio Miss Liebling puts the female contingent of the Liebling Singers through their 1948 pretour paces. I'm the blonde in the center. The gal on my left is Susie Yager Cook, my oldest, dearest friend and my daughter Muffy's godmother.

4

Tired, hoarse,
running a high fever,
I can always sing Violetta

My first Violetta—on tour
with the Wagner Company, 1951.

Miss Liebling, I must say, didn't take long to come up with something—through another great and good friend, of course. Désiré Defrère, a stage director at the Metropolitan Opera, was then preparing to take on tour an opera company organized by Charles Wagner, one of the all-time great impresarios, who launched the careers of so many artists that it would be impossible to list them. Wagner's touring company was the only one of its kind in the United States at that time; in nine weeks it used to do a series of sixty-three one-night stands with a thirty-piece orchestra and two alternating casts.

Miss Liebling got Defrère to come to her studio to hear me sing, he got Mr. Wagner to let me audition for him, *et voilà!* I was launched. To my amazement, Mr. Wagner offered me the role of Violetta in *La Traviata;* he was the first impresario to tell me, "Miss Sills, you are going to be a star." Many years later, in 1975, when I made my debut at the Met, Francis Robinson, the assistant manager, gave me an opening night gift of a photograph showing Charles Wagner with one of the other artists he had once handled—

Amelita Galli-Curci. Robinson knew how great an influence they both had been in my life.

That tour in 1951 began my operatic career. I sang more than forty Violettas. I have sung more than three hundred Violettas since but the basis of my characterization is still the one Defrère taught me on the tour. I would experiment with the character, never playing her the same way twice, and when I finished the tour I could sing Violetta standing on my head or doing somersaults. To this day, sick, tired, hoarse, or running a high fever, I can always sing Violetta. She has been trained into my vocal chords.

Defrère was with us on all sixty-three nights. Every morning after a performance he would call me to the front of the bus we traveled in—he had a double seat to himself while the rest of us shared—and for an hour we would discuss my performance the day before, why I had done this or that, try it this way tomorrow. Once he gave me a pair of rhinestone earrings that he had bought in the previous town. "Put these on tomorrow in the first act," he said, "but do the third act with no jewelry at all." "After all," he explained, "the invitation Violetta receives for the party in Paris comes *after* she has already sold all her jewelry to support Alfredo and herself in the country." Defrère challenged me constantly on my characterization of Violetta.

On that tour we would travel three hundred miles a day on the bus, arrive at a town, race through dinner, get into costume in a dressing room if there was one or in the bus if there was not. Alfredo was sung by a then unknown tenor named John Alexander. To while away the time on the bus John taught me to play poker. He considered himself a real shark, but by the time the tour was over he owed me $132. We were inseparable; that is, when he wasn't writing love letters (he wrote a lot) to his fiancée, Susie, whom he later married. We were earning only $75 per performance. The first order of business in any new town was to search out the cheapest café. We would insist on seeing the most expensive steak in the joint, usually about $1.50. If it was big enough to split two ways, we would order one; if it wasn't, we would complain about the steak, send it back, and order something cheaper. Everything that came with the dinner we gobbled up; whatever we weren't able to eat on the spot we would take back to the hotel. Everyone on the tour traveled with his own portable cooking equipment. You would walk down the halls and smell the most delicious garlic butter sauce. Sometimes there were spaghetti parties: we would each chip in twenty-five cents and somebody in the chorus would run out to buy spaghetti, cheap red wine, and Italian bread.

John Alexander is my oldest, dearest tenor friend. I think I have sung more performances with him than with any other man. In March of 1976, when we sang *Traviata* together at the Met, the audience tossed confetti and flowers at us and I turned to John on the stage, kissed him, and said, "We've certainly come a long way from the Wagner tour!" We both got teary-eyed right there.

I came back from that first Wagner tour a far more sophisticated singer than when I had left. My voice was still that of a twenty-one-year-old girl but the performer, the actress, had matured a great deal. I now had an idea of who I was on the stage and a passionate urge to make the public pay attention to me. It had been a kind of evolutionary process—finishing off with people like Annini in Philadelphia, Max de Rieux, in Paris and now Defrère on tour.

Defrère was a very amusing, charming man. He believed in my talent. He also loved my mother. He thought she was the most beautiful woman he had ever seen and he would constantly tease her to marry him so that I would have a permanent stage director and never have to shop around for one. He was extremely thoughtful and generous. He bought me the first illustrated classic I had ever read, Anatole France's *Thaïs*. More important, he emphasized to me that whenever one plays a role based on a figure in literature, it is wise to read the literature first. I have always followed that advice—going back to the original Lucia, the original Traviata, the original Manon. I have found it the ideal way of gaining insight into a character that is perhaps not so obvious in the treatment given it by the composer. Defrère gave me two other pieces of sound advice: Eat steak and salad at four P.M. on the day of a performance (I still do). And don't worry about short tenors: that's not your problem, he would say, it's the tenor's (I don't worry any more).

I still have a great many opera scores bearing little scribbled sketches by Defrère. Some of the operas I had never seen performed and in his drawings of the stage sets for them he would always draw, right in the middle, a caricature of me with very curly hair looking like Harpo Marx. I loved to telephone him just to hear him shriek my name. He pronounced Beverly as though it had ninety-six syllables.

When I was married, Defrère was the only person from my theatrical world, other than Miss Liebling, whom I wanted at the ceremony. He was then quite old, still playing the nice-dirty-old-man role. He toasted my mother: "Shirley, you're not losing a daughter today, you're gaining a husband, ME." The day Miss Liebling and I learned that he had died, we looked at each other without a word. A bright color had gone out of our lives.

After that Wagner tour I had to struggle again. I did a few recitals early in 1952. I acquired an agent and was invited to sing with the St. Louis Symphony. John Alexander and I did a concert version of *Traviata* in Vermont —$100. I began singing on the Borscht Belt; the Concord Hotel in the Catskills had opera nights every Tuesday and many famous opera singers would appear there. I would do several arias backed by Sholom Secunda's orchestra and I would come home with $90, which went a long way in those days. The huge rooms were packed with appreciative Jews, the food was fantastic, and I got to sing a lot of my high notes—not a bad way to spend an evening.

In September of that year I went on tour with Mr. Wagner's company again, this time as Micaela in *Carmen*. I wound up doing sixty-three Micaelas on the tour, and even the money—$100 per performance—did not entirely make up for the loss of my sanity. Micaela is *not* one of my favorite roles; it is limited and frustrating, a bore.

Still, aside from the money, there were compensations. I took up the classical guitar. I learned every role in *Carmen;* I can sing the opera from the first note to the last and could even conduct it, I think. I did a lot of reading—Oscar Wilde, Hemingway, loads of plays. Reading was a very costly hobby for me—in those days there were few paperbacks. I used to buy a hardcover book in one city, read it all day on the bus, sell it in the next city to a used-book store, and with the money buy another new book. I learned to play chess—Defrère taught me but he was a terrible cheat—and bridge—my brother had taught me that game the year before and I began to read books on the subject.

When the tour was over, I was twenty-three years old, had more than

A scene from my first Traviata *with the Wagner Touring Company. My tenor friend John Alexander, playing Alfredo, is seated at the table behind me. Last year, when I went to Memphis to sing* La Traviata, *a girl from the chorus walked on stage wearing that same dress; it had been preserved and refurbished from the time I wore it when I was twenty-one and had been in use for twenty-five more years. I recognized it because it still had the red thread I had used to sew on the turquoise velvet fringes. The fan dangling from my wrist is the same fan I use today in the role.*

a hundred opera performances under my belt—and was out of a job again. The Wagner tour the following year would be *Madama Butterfly*, an opera that was not and is not in my repertoire. It is too heavy a role for my voice and I have always felt that someone with my figure would look ridiculous trying to play a little Japanese girl. I would probably be billed as "The Biggest Butterfly In Captivity." Besides, I felt that two tours with Wagner were enough. I wanted to move on to something new.

Désiré Defrère (above) was my mentor on those two Wagner tours. For my third-act Violetta (right) his instructions were formal: painted eyebrows, dark red lips, but no jewelry and no false eyelashes. He thought false eyelashes changed the entire look of a face. I do wear them in the role now but whenever I do, I think, Oh, D.D. wouldn't like this.

As Micaela in Carmen *during the second Wagner tour, in 1952. You can tell from the sweet boredom on my face how I feel about Micaela.*

About to embark on my first opera tour with the Wagner Company in 1951. My outfit was made, like all my things then, by my mother. That handsome purse I'm clutching was bought for fifty cents in Rio de Janeiro when I was on that Moore-McCormack trip. The little ring on my pinkie was a good-luck present from my mother; I still have it. The white-haired gentleman holding my hand is impresario Charles Wagner. Standing over him is tenor John Alexander and next to John is baritone Ed Dunning.

5

*I was still saying "yes"
to everything*

My first Manon, 1953.

Maestro Bamboschek, my old friend from the Philadelphia Opera Company, had nothing for me when I phoned, but *his* old friend, Rosa Ponselle, was forming a company in Baltimore with *Manon* in the repertoire and maybe, he said, she might have something. He arranged an audition for me and Miss Ponselle sent her chauffeur to drive me from the railroad station to her home, the Villa Pace. When I saw it I said to myself, *That's* the kind of home a prima donna should have. It was an Italian villa that she had had brought over from Italy brick by brick. It had oodles of poodles yapping all over the property, lots of servants, a swimming pool, acres of landscaped grounds. At the doorway stood Rosa herself, robed in a stunning caftan.

When I walked through that door we became instant lifetime friends; the chemistry was incredible. She threw her arms around me, gave me a big bunny hug and a glass of wine. I had come prepared to stay one day; I stayed five. I walked into a house that had all the atmosphere of glamour and wealth, everything I had dreamed of, yet here was this simple, down-to-earth, warm lady with an enormous ringing laugh. In her closet were fur coats as far as the eye could see, and she would ever so casually stick her hand inside, pull out a mink, and drape me in it; then we would walk through the woods in the stinging cold.

Rosa would sing for me anything that came into her head—Isolde, Manon. Although I have always been very skeptical when people say you should have heard so-and-so sing in the so-called "Golden Age," her voice *was* still in its golden age. I have never heard another voice like it. Her face is extremely broad between the cheekbones—the area that singers call the "mask"—and her whole voice seemed miraculously to sit up in that mask. It was spine-tingling, hearing that voice in her great villa.

I sang parts of *Manon* for her and she was a most considerate listener—more than that, a most considerate colleague. I was, after all, just a kid of twenty-three; nobody knew what hole in the wall I had come out of. And she was the famous Rosa Ponselle. Yet the relationship between us was that of two colleagues and she made me feel unique. Three hours after my arrival we were chattering away about the characterization of Manon, arguing over it. (Needless to say, I got the part!) Everyone I had ever worked with on Manon before—people such as de Rieux and Defrère—had always discussed the role as played in the French light style. But Rosa, who was the artistic director for the new Baltimore Opera and had much to do with working on characterizations, especially with new young people, saw Manon differently. For her, the role should be played much more in the exaggerated Italian *verismo* style. We quarreled and quibbled over the interpretation; I had envisioned Manon in a totally different way. But ours was a very stimulating collaboration and it served to rid me of some of my inhibitions. What I had learned from Defrère on any interpretation was never really the result of mutual give-and-take; it was simply instructions from him and I had never challenged them. Rosa had never portrayed Manon but she was a performer, and so our tug-of-war was a creative exercise for me.

Whatever the reasons, *Manon* was a huge success in Baltimore. I played her in the early scenes as though she were a little girl from the countryside who had got caught in the hayloft a few times too many by her parents and as a result was being rushed off to a convent, a girl with a voluptuous figure who had not yet learned how to show it off, who exuded a lot of sex appeal but no polish. My entrance was, and still is, in flat-heeled shoes as a kind of flat-footed country bumpkin with a knack for attracting men. Not till later in the opera did I turn Manon into the graceful, beautiful courtesan.

After that Baltimore engagement I was somewhat depressed because I had not realized completely the Manon I had wanted. But I knew now that I was a good actress and I felt I had finally made it. After my first Charles Wagner tour I had expected that all New York would be waiting for me; I thought that everyone knew about my triumph in Athens, Georgia, and how the critic in Kansas City had called me "The Singing Bernhardt." I had assumed that all doors to the operatic stage would be open to me. They were not, of course. But now, after Baltimore, my getting to know Rosa Ponselle had made me a part of the real scene. I was very aware that unlike Mary Garden and Geraldine Ferrar, who had built their reputations abroad before singing here, Rosa was an all-American girl from Meriden, Connecticut, who had made it big here right from the start. And she was my friend, my Rosa. I began to feel that, finally, I belonged to the world of opera. There were a handful of people, at least, who knew what a Beverly Sills was.

Soon after I did *Manon* in Baltimore, Charles Wagner wrote a letter about me to Gaetano Merola, music director of the San Francisco Opera Company. So did Miss Liebling. The twin salvo may have seemed to Mr. Merola a tactical bombardment, but it wasn't planned that way. I didn't even know about the letters. In any case, when Mr. Merola came to New York early in 1953, I sang for him. He went into shock when I told him the number of operas I knew and how many performances I had already done. The upshot was that he invited me to come to San Francisco that summer and live with him and his wife while he coached me in the roles I would do that fall in repertory. My debut was to be as Elena (Helen of Troy) in Boito's *Mefistofele*, but my big plum would be the role of Donna Elvira in Mozart's *Don Giovanni*. I was, as you can imagine, terribly excited; I had the world on my string.

Mr. Merola had written me that I would be met at the San Francisco airport and taken to his home, but when I arrived with my two suitcases there was nobody there to meet me. I couldn't reach him by phone, the line was always busy. When I finally made it to his home by public transportation, I found chaos: Mr. Merola had died the night before, while conducting a performance. His wife was not to be seen, of course, and nobody seemed to know who I was or that I was expected. I took my two suitcases and went to the opera house. There they knew who I was but not what to do with me. I wound up at a terrible hotel on Market Street but at least it was cheap; I didn't have much cash on me because I had been expecting to move in with the Merolas, and I did not want to impose on my mother to send me money. I figured that I could last it out until I went into official rehearsal and on the payroll the following week. I knew no one in town and I didn't eat very much for several days. It was the loneliest week I have ever spent; for a long time afterwards, whenever I heard the name San Francisco I would feel cold shivers up and down my spine, remembering.

But finally rehearsals began (Kurt Adler having been appointed acting artistic director), and I found a little apartment in a hotel. We began to plan for my mother to come out to live with me. Things were looking up. The conductor for *Mefistofele* was Fausto Cleva. At the first rehearsal he asked me if I spoke Italian. When I said yes, he laid me out in lavender—in Italian— for having agreed to do a role meant for a dramatic soprano voice when I was a lyric coloratura. The best careers, he yelled, were the result of learning to say no, I should never have accepted the role. But as soon as I explained to him that it had been Mr. Merola's idea, not mine, he relented. Later, when anyone in the cast became sick and he felt that I could substitute in the role, he would call on me. He would continue to yell at me, of course, that I wasn't doing it correctly, do this, do that, picky-picky-picky. But underneath it all I think he really liked me; he became a great pal and helped me a good deal.

My debut as Helen of Troy was extremely successful. So was my appearance as Donna Elvira, although the production was a little disappointing for me. The conductor was Tullio Serafin and I had looked forward to working with him, but I think that I came into his life a few years too late. He was by then old (seventy-five) and tired; he conducted as though he didn't care very much.

One night, on very short notice, I was thrown into a performance of Wagner's *Die Walküre* as a substitute for a singer who had left the company because her father was ill. The role was Gerhilde, one of those eight lady Valkyries dressed in robes, shields, breastplates, and helmets shouting "Hoyotoho, Hoyotoho" from the balcony. In the excitement of my being a last-minute replacement on opening night, nobody remembered to try the helmet on me for size—although everything else including the great breast-plate (you should pardon the expression) had been altered to fit me. Natu-rally, during the performance my helmet fell off and clattered to the foot-lights. I should have left it there, but instead I darted over to retrieve it while the audience clapped its approval. Seventeen years later, when I returned to the San Francisco Opera to sing again, there was my helmet filled with fruit, nuts, a big bottle of wine, and a card that said "Welcome Home." Kurt Adler had dug up the old helmet; it still said "Sills" in it. Now it sits in my living room in New York, a plant holder.

San Francisco was good experience for me. It was, and still is, one of the finest opera companies in the United States. I got to do four different roles—including the fifth slave girl in *Elektra*. I came away with wonderful personal notices. I met a great many famous people and sang with them. On evenings when I wasn't singing I would listen to others: Cesare Valetti and Giulietta Simionato in *Werther*; Simionato again in *Barber of Seville*. I heard Alba-nese's Butterfly and wept and wept and wept. I heard Inge Borkh's Elektra—hair-raising.

And I made more lifetime friendships. One I especially cherish was with Italo Tajo, who sang Leporello with me in *Don Giovanni*. Before my mother got to San Francisco, Italo knew how lonely I was. He helped me find my apartment and made sure I never had to eat lunch or dinner alone. He took me to Fisherman's Wharf. He was the perfect escort, amusing and cultivated. Today he and his wife, Inelda, live in Cincinnati, where he is Professor of Voice and Opera at the University of Cincinnati Conservatory of Music.

Even if years go by without our getting together, when we do meet we pick up the conversation right where we left off in mid-sentence. The warm affection that we felt in San Francisco I still feel—for him and Inelda.

When I returned to New York in December of 1953, Maestro Bamboschek introduced me to Carlo Vinti, who was then producing a television show on Dumont Television called "Opera Cameo." The sponsors were Progresso Foods and Gallo Wines, and in addition to singing three operas I did commercials for antipasto, minestrone, and Gallo's California Tawny Port. If you think that last item is easy to say, try it a few times. I sang my first *Tosca*, with Giovanni Martinelli narrating the story act by act for the TV audience. Probably no one understood his English but it didn't matter, he was such a presence with that shock of white hair, like the King of the Beasts. I did *Traviata* with the great baritone Ettore Bastianini; he courted me with parakeets that he had trained to say *Bella, Bella, Bella*. I also sang *Thaïs*; how *that* French dish got into all that Italianate fare I do not know. I wound up with barrels of Gallo wine and cases of Progresso food. I'm not sure that I ever got paid any money but the exposure was fabulous—all the television time plus reams of publicity in the Italian-language newspaper *Il Progresso*. And after every show Mr. Vinti, whose whole family seemed to be working on the program, would take me home, where his wife Rosa would put out a spread of Italian food that could have fed the whole Italian army. *Bella, bella, bella*, indeed!

That summer, 1954, I went to Salt Lake City to sing, of all things, *Aida*. I had not yet accepted Maestro Cleva's advice—that the best careers come when one learns to say no. I was still saying yes to everything because I needed to earn a living and because I felt that the more people who heard me sing, the better. Besides, Salt Lake, although a huge outdoor stadium, had lots of microphones, which meant I would not have to strain my voice. All I had to do was look the part. Perhaps I did, and I sang Aida well, I think—no Leontyne Price but it was musical and I enjoyed it.

All in all, I was beginning to get somewhere. At least I was singing a good many performances. The time was now right, Miss Liebling decided, to make a serious assault on another bastion—the New York City Opera.

Opening night of **Manon**, Baltimore, 1953. At left,
backstage with my mother, who made all my
costumes for the opera, including the ones
hanging behind us. Above, Rosa Ponselle and I,
radiant at the post-opera party. Below, Mama and
I flank Maestro Bamboschek and his wife.

*Playing a scene with Italo Tajo at the
San Francisco Opera's 1953 production of
Don Giovanni—he Leporello, me Donna
Elvira. Nicola Rossi-Lemini was Giovanni
and Jan Peerce was Don Ottavio.*

In the summer of 1953 I sang Traviata *and*
Naughty Marietta *in Brigham Young
Stadium with the Salt Lake City Orchestra,
conducted by Maurice Abravanel. This is a
dress rehearsal of* Traviata *with me,
Violetta, greeting my guests. The stage was
so big we needed twenty-four microphones
to be heard.*

In 1954, my days of wine and minestrone—singing opera and doing commercials for Progresso Foods and other Italian outfits on a TV program called "Opera Cameo." At left, whipping up a salad commercial. Below, left, dressed up for my role as Tosca with leading man Jon Crain; we were to sing together later at the New York City Opera. Below, discussing my Tosca role with producer Carlo Vinti. And finally (bottom, opposite page) my interpretation of Thaïs—and my mother's (she made the costume).

is Aida, believe it or not,
lt Lake City, 1954.

At my San Francisco Opera debut in 1953 as
Helen of Troy. I am congratulated by an admirer.

59

6

*Mama, Mama,
I think I've met a man
I could marry*

No personality, Dr. Rosenstock said.

At twenty-five I was a rather *zaftig* redhead and I liked to show off my figure by wearing very low-cut gowns. But for auditions I felt that my image as a serious opera singer called for a more sedate, proper look—the simple black dress, long red hair tied in a tight bun, hands clasped demurely beneath ample bosom, et cetera. That is the look I adopted when I began auditioning for Dr. Joseph Rosenstock, who was then the general manager of the New York City Opera in the old City Center on Fifty-fifth Street. Since 1952 I had auditioned for him seven times and got nowhere. When my agent asked me to do just one more audition for him in 1955, I said, Why keep going back, why not just ask him what's wrong? "I did," my agent said. "He says, 'She has a phenomenal voice but no personality.' "

I nearly exploded. I went to that final audition, in the spring of 1953, with an enormous chip on my shoulder. I wore black lace stockings and a dress cut nearly to the navel, and I let my hair hang all the way down. When I walked on stage, Dr. Rosenstock, who I later learned was a long-time afficionado of ladies' legs, came down the aisle, looked closely at me, and said in his heavy German accent, "Vell, vell, and vat are ve going to sing today?" "Well, Dr. Rosenstock," I replied, rather icily, "you've already heard *my* entire repertoire so I think I'll start on somebody else's. I will sing '*La Mamma Morta,*' from *Andrea Chenier.*"

To sing an aria for dramatic soprano in my high, light coloratura voice was, of course, ridiculous; I was a guppy pretending to be a whale. When I had finished, Dr. Rosenstock just smiled and asked, "Vat else do you vant to sing?" "Actually," I replied, "I don't really want to sing anything for you, but if you want more, I'll do '*Vissi d'arte,*' from *Tosca*"—another dramatic soprano role.

"Okay, Sills," Dr. Rosenstock said after my second number, "upstairs to my office, you've got yourself a chob." It must have been the black-laced legs. He offered me a debut the following season in the role of Rosalinda in *Die Fledermaus* and also an understudy role in Tchaikovsky's *The Golden Slipper* (later affectionately called by the cast *The Golden Schlepper*). I was ecstatic—not only at the $75 per performance but at the prospect of a New York debut and the chance to be part of a company that included Norman Treigle, Cornell MacNeil, Frances Bible, Eva Likova, Virginia Haskins—some pretty damned good singers! And there was also Julius Rudel, then Rosenstock's assistant—"Chulyuss," he would scream at the top of his lungs. During all my auditions at the City Center Julius was the friendly face in the back of the house, and he always had something pleasant to say to me before I went on.

My debut in *Die Fledermaus* in October 1955 was, thank God, a great success. The role of my on-stage lover, Alfred, was played by Jon Crain, with whom I had done a TV "Opera Cameo" production of *Tosca;* he was the funniest Alfred I ever saw or sang with in my life. Coley Worth, who played the jailer, was always up to some unscripted mischief on stage and you had to be on guard when you played a scene with him. I was wearing a low-cut gown and high heels and to heighten the glamorous look I was carrying a king-sized, filter-tipped cigarette that had just been introduced on the market. Coley looked at me, then turned to the audience. "King-sized, eh?"

Then, looking down the front of my dress, "And filter-tipped too." The audience broke up and so did I.

Later in that first season I got a chance to sing Oxana in *The Golden Slipper*. The company was committed to do three performances of the Tchaikovsky work, and after the first two—not very successful—Jean Fenn moved out of the role and I was pushed in for the third. The lead tenor was Richard Cassilly, who later became the leading tenor of the Hamburg Opera. (He left the United States because he couldn't support his family as a singer here; the Hamburg Opera at least had a medical and pension plan, unlike opera houses in this country.) I was delighted to be singing with Cassilly: he was six feet four, and despite Defrère's advice I was still worrying about playing opposite short tenors. So much so that I had earlier written a poem to Julius Rudel:

> I'd like a tenor taller than my ass-illy.
> Please, Chulyuss Darlink, can I have Dick Cass-illy?

Since all the rest of Miss Fenn's costumes for the part of Oxana fitted me, I hadn't bothered to try on her golden slippers. That was a mistake. At the climax of the opera, the tenor brings in the slippers—all I can remember about Oxana is that she keeps singing about four million times, "Bring me the golden slipper and we shall be married"—and puts them on Oxana's feet; the couple does a lovely dance, sings a marvelous duet, and lives happily ever after. Jean's feet, it turned out, were slightly larger than mine; the slippers went on very easily but they came off the same way. I danced right out of the shoes. When the curtain came down, there I was barefoot while the golden slippers sat prominently on stage with no feet in them.

It was one of my less triumphant evenings in the theater. Dick Cassilly and I never stopped laughing until it was time for curtain calls. But backstage I could hear that familiar Rosenstock shriek—SILLS!—and I knew I was in for it. Rosenstock refused to take my hand during curtain calls and it was a long time before he would even speak to me again. Nevertheless, he rehired me for the 1956 season. I have been with the New York City Opera ever since.

Dr. Rosenstock was a very volatile man with a difficult job and I learned a great deal working with him. We later became good friends, although he never called me anything but SILLS! When anyone in the company was too ill to go on, he would always say, "Get Sills, Sills will do it." He knew exactly the type of voice I had and tried to find the right roles for me in the coloratura repertoire. Not an easy task: the City Opera in those days chose the operas first and the singers for them second, not the other way round.

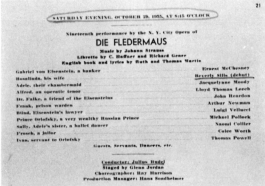

Dr. Joseph Rosenstock hired me in 1955 to sing with the New York City Opera and I made my debut in October as Rosalinda in Die Fledermaus.

As Rosalinda (left) in my City Opera debut. My mother made the gown (in those days the opera was more than grateful if a singer could provide her own costume!). The fan I picked up for a dollar at the Paris flea market. The earrings were the same rhinestone jobs that Defrère had given me on that 1952 Traviata *tour. I also wore a white stole Mama and I found at a thrift shop. At far right, a scene from the opera, with Jon Crain playing the part of my lover, Alfred.*

In 1964, when the New York City Opera revived Die Fledermaus, *it was in good enough financial shape so that Mama didn't have to make my costumes. At right, that's John Reardon as Alfred; I've sung a great many operas with him and he later joined the Met. Below, Jon Crain (in the stocking cap) is Alfred and Lee Cass is the prison warden.*

In the summer of 1955, while awaiting my City Opera debut that fall, I sang the lead in the Cleveland Music Carnival's production of Rosalinda, *a sort of Broadway version of* Die Fledermaus.

In those days, too, the City Opera did only a fall season, no spring; instead, the company would tour the provinces. One night, while we were on tour in Cleveland, the company threw a party for the local press. I did not want to go—I wanted instead to see a movie entitled "The Man Who Loved Redheads"—but Julius Rudel insisted that I attend the party. So I did—in a very low-cut dress indeed. At my table was a handsome blond man who began winking at me. Well, *that's* a novel approach, I thought. Then the man passed me a book of matches on which he had scribbled his telephone number and a note saying that if I had any free time he would like to see me. Come to the party being thrown for me tomorrow night, I said, after my performance in *Die Fledermaus*. I can't, he said, I have another date. That's too bad, I said, and left the party and went to the movies.

The next night the big handsome blond man showed up at the party; he had got rid of his date, he said, because he wanted to see me again. His name was Peter Greenough, he was an associate editor of a local newspaper, the *Cleveland Plain Dealer*, which was then owned by his family, and would I have dinner with him tomorrow night—Sunday? Can't, I said, I'm going beagling during the day and then back home; my mother expects me.

While beagling—in Cleveland they do it on horseback and I felt like Auntie Mame—I must admit that I thought about Peter a great deal. I was supposed to catch a six P.M. flight to New York. What possessed me I don't know, but instead of taking that flight I phoned the big handsome blond man and said that dinner would be fine. Then I phoned my mother to break the news that I was going to spend the night in Cleveland; I was tired from horseback riding, and so on. I think she suspected something but she didn't pursue it on the phone.

When I came down to the hotel lobby to meet the big handsome blond man, he had two cute little girls with him. One was Lindley, aged nine, the other was Nancy, six. They're mine, he said. Where's the mama? I asked. Right at the moment, he said, I don't know. We dropped the subject, what with the children standing there, climbed into his station wagon, and drove to his home—which seemed miles and miles and hours and hours away. Later, when we were married and I had moved into that home, I realized it was only about eight minutes from downtown Cleveland but at the time I thought that he was taking me into the wilderness. Why in hell did I ever agree to *this?* I began thinking. Who is this guy, anyway, what is this with his kids, he doesn't even know where his wife is, and this is the dumbest move I have ever made.

Peter's home was a beautiful twenty-five-room French château on Lake Erie in a community called Bratenahl. Inside the house were two lovely ladies and a Chinese supper. One lady served supper and disappeared and afterwards the other lady disappeared with the two nice children. That left Peter Greenough and little Beverly Sills sitting in this living room, which was probably forty-five by thirty feet, in front of an enormous fireplace. Well, dummy, I said to myself, you've finally done it.

In his best Rudolph Valentino manner Peter put a Frank Sinatra record on the hi-fi—"One for My Baby, and One for the Road." Then he asked, Shall I light a fire? It seemed logical—this was Cleveland in November. But Peter had just moved into the house, the fireplace had never been lit before, and he forgot to heat up the chimney first to induce a draft. What was supposed to be a rather romantic production turned into an unromantic asphyxiation; the smoke that poured from the fireplace almost choked me to death. We wound up opening all the windows and retreating to his kitchen, where we talked for hours. Peter was originally from Boston, a direct descendant of John Alden, one of the Mayflower's passengers; another ancestor, the first Peter Bulkeley here, had founded the town of Concord, Massachusetts. He was in the process of divorcing his wife and trying to get custody of their three children. He asked me if he could come to New York to see me and I said yes. Then he took me to the hotel and picked me up again several hours later to take me to the airport for the nine o'clock flight to New York.

When I got home, the first thing my mother asked was, all right, why the delay in coming back? "Mama, Mama," I said happily, "I think I've met a man I could marry." My mother was ecstatic—at first; I was, after all, twenty-six years old and in Jewish families mothers have long since begun to despair when their babies reach that age unmarried. (Not that I had been a shrinking violet: I had so many dates between Sandy Levine and Peter Greenough that they all now seem one big blur. My brothers used to fix me up with college friends of theirs, both Jewish and non-Jewish; some of them were even *doctors!* I was the kind of girl that men seemed to get serious about quickly, but until Peter came along I never got really serious about any of them.)

Back to Peter.

"There's a small problem, though, Mama," I said. "What is it, sweetheart?" "He's still married," I said, "he has three children, he's thirteen years older than I, and he's not Jewish." Mama burst into tears: "Why does everything have to happen to my baby?"

Peter was very clever. He knew that there would be tremendous resistance from my family, especially from my mother, and so he set about to make her an ally. Whenever he came to New York, he wooed both of us, bringing Mama flowers and books. We became a sort of *ménage à trois:* it was always Mama, Peter, and Bubbles because Mama was not about to allow her baby girl to be seen in public, unchaperoned, with a married man. We had wonderful times together—the three of us. One night Peter and I had a terrible row, much to my mother's embarrassment and discomfort, and he turned to me and said, "You know, I think I'm gonna marry your mother instead, she's so much nicer."

My mother and I were still living in that tiny two-room apartment in Stuyvesant Town, and once Peter overdid the flowers-for-Mama bit. He bought her an azalea tree that kept growing and growing. It stood in the middle of the living room, so big that it was impossible for two people to sit at opposite sides of the room and see each other without moving the tree. Whenever Mama and I wanted to talk, we had to huddle together on the sofa or else keep moving the tree around. It didn't survive all that schlepping but

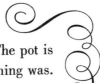

to this day my mother has refused to get rid of the pot it came in. The pot is now an umbrella holder—which gives you an idea of how big the thing was.

On New Year's Day, 1956, I received a phone call from Maestro Bamboschek in Philadelphia: Vivian della Chiesa was scheduled to sing Montemezzi's *The Love of Three Kings* but she was ill, could I learn the opera in eight days? Could I! I could have learned it in eight hours, it was such an opportunity. The role of Fiora is a beautiful one—Lucrezia Bori had made it one of her jewels—and to sing with the tenor Ramon Vinay was a soprano's dream. Peter was visiting the apartment when I got the phone call and the next day he bought me a recording of the opera. By dress rehearsal time on January 7 I had memorized the role and two days later I performed it.

The production attracted a great deal of attention because the opera was rarely performed, and I received an excellent reception from press and public. Fernando Corena sang the basso role of King Archibaldo, Fiora's father-in-law. In the opera Corena had to lift my "dead" body from a bench and carry me across the stage of the Philadelphia Academy of Music to an upstage exit. Corena, though a well-built fellow, was not very big. To this day, when we spot each other on a street he will yell, *"Ciao, Bella,"* then grab his side and double over in pretended agony. He tells everyone that I caused him the one and only hernia of his life—jokingly, of course.

That summer I was engaged by the Music Carnival in Cleveland to sing Carmen, *not* Micaela but Carmen, a role I had never sung before. It was ideal timing, not only because of the cast—Norman Treigle as the toreador, Lloyd Thomas Leech as Don José—but also because Peter lived there. I sang eighteen Carmens on eighteen successive nights, which must be some kind of record. I took all the high endings Bizet had written and loved every minute of it. In my interpretation I used a good deal of the "business" Defrère and I had discussed during those long bus rides on the Wagner tours. For example, when Carmen is tied up and left in Don José's custody, he throws her into a chair and she casually crosses her legs. At this point Defrère would have Carmen, whose hands are tied behind her back, bend over and with her teeth pull up her skirts to expose more of her legs and further excite Don José.

Treigle, too, had invented a piece of business. When, as the toreador, he sees Carmen for the first time, he is eating an orange. He would swagger over to me, look insinuatingly at my bosom, and say, "I'd like to be a friend of yours." "You already have enough friends," Carmen would reply. He, still staring at the bosom, replies, "Yes, but I want to be a *very* good friend." And then he would take a big bite of the orange. The audience loved it, as did Norman.

Norman and I, both new to the New York City Opera, were already good friends, very eager to work together. We were both riding high in those days, having the time of our lives. I had promised my mother that Peter and I would not be seen alone together in Cleveland, so Peter, Norman, and I soon became a trio. The two men got along so well that occasionally they forgot I was there. I spent a lot of time with Peter's daughters, Lindley and Nancy. Peter and I felt that it would be good for me to get to know them better because it was beginning to look as though he would get them in the divorce settlement. His third daughter, Diana, his youngest and a retarded child, was away at a special school and I didn't meet her until after Peter and I were married.

We became formally engaged shortly after Peter got his divorce in early October. Mama had insisted that we wait six weeks before we got married; what that magic number was supposed to mean I do not know, but she seemed to feel that it wasn't right to marry any sooner after Peter's divorce. We settled for a big engagement party in Cleveland.

When Peter was courting me, my mother used to tease me. "How big an engagement diamond are you getting?" she would ask. "How big did you have?" I replied. "Three carats." "Okay," I said, "so I'll have three carats too." Until the day Peter gave me my engagement ring he and I had a kind of a game. Every time we separated he would hold up two fingers—one for

each carat—and I would hold up three. Then one day he stepped from an airplane and held up three fingers.

The announcement that a nice middle-class Jewish girl from Brooklyn named Beverly Sills was engaged to a rich Boston Brahmin named Peter Bulkeley Greenough must have puzzled a good many people. One of them was a little Jewish shopkeeper who lived in our Stuyvesant Town neighborhood. Originally from Odessa, Russia, where my mother was born, he would always chat with her in Russian; his only English came from a diligent reading of every word of the Sunday *New York Times*. When he read my engagement announcement in the paper he said to my mother, "Nu? I read she's getting married. Greenough? Greenough? What kind of name is Greenough?" "He's a wonderful boy," my mother said. "Greenough?" the little Jewish shopkeeper continued. "He must have changed his name from Greenbaum." Now, whenever I get angry with Peter I say, "Look here, Peter Greenbaum."

I was then under the management of National Concerts and Artists Corporation and not very happy about it. They had swallowed up my two former agents and I felt like a small fish in a large pond. They were not paying much attention to my career (there were so many more famous artists they were already handling), and so I decided I needed a change in management. At the time Leonard Bernstein was conducting a concert performance of *Der Rosenkavalier* with the NBC Symphony Orchestra in New York. I auditioned for the role of the Marschallin; Lenny offered me Sophie instead and he was absolutely right. *Time* magazine gave me a rave review complete with photograph, but the caption indicated that I was more interested in a career than in marriage. Naturally, that made Peter tremendously angry with the NCAC people, who had apparently been interviewed for the *Time* story. Although Peter has always made it a policy not to interfere in my career matters, I knew he was offended. Then at our engagement party an executive of NCAC asked my mother, Why does she have to marry him, why doesn't she get engaged to him for a few years and then she can get engaged to someone else?—implying that anything permanent at this point in my life could mean the end of my career.

That did it: NCAC had now made two enemies, my husband-to-be *and* my mother. I left them. Julius Rudel then recommended me to Columbia Artists Management; they kept me waiting in an outside hall for two hours and finally a man said, "Well, we have a stableful of sopranos already just like you. *I* said, "I'm not a horse, and even if I were, I still wouldn't want to be in your stable." At various times in my career I had noticed a gentleman named Ludwig Lustig, an agent who used to come backstage to wish his clients luck. I thought that very sweet. I went to see Mr. Lustig; we signed and have been together ever since.

That season with the City Opera I repeated Rosalinda but I was also given two new roles. One was Madame Goldentrill in *The Impresario,* Mozart's one-act opera. That gave me my first chance really to sing coloratura, with several high Fs to negotiate. It was also a very comic role and I enjoyed it thoroughly. For the first time my picture was published in a New York newspaper—a very exciting first.

By then Dr. Rosenstock and I had a kind of teasing relationship. He was small, I was large, and he did not like to stand next to me too often. He would tease me about my size and because he was the boss I could never tease him back. But *The Impresario* gave me an opportunity. In it, two sopranos, one an established primadonna (Mme. Goldentrill) and the other a young poopsie (Mme. Silverpeal), vie to prove who can sing higher. When I was ready to begin my aria I was supposed to pull out a large purple handkerchief and wave it at the conductor, Dr. Rosenstock, to cue him and the orchestra. Every time I played the role, I kept delaying the cue, always finding more stage business to prolong it until Dr. Rosenstock was a nervous wreck. When I finally gave him the cue, he would look up at me with an expression that said, "Vait, I'll get you ven this opera is over."

The other new role I sang that season was Philine in Ambroise Thomas's *Mignon.* For the first time in New York I felt that I had a role ideally suited to my voice and temperament—a glamorous part in which I could both speak and sing in French. It was a very difficult opera to do, particularly with an all-American cast (Frances Bible was Mignon and Donald Gramm, Laertes). Jean Morel, the conductor, coached me in the role; he was so pleased that I could speak French with him that whenever I made a mistake during the staging or did anything to displease him, he would look at me and say, "Et tu, Philine," as though I were Brutus and had just betrayed his Caesar. When I sang my coloratura showpiece, *"Je Suis Titania,"* it brought down the house, the first time I had caused *that* to happen. Because of the audience reaction, the excellent reviews, and Mr. Morel's enthusiasm about my contribution to *Mignon,* I thought that this was, finally, it—the successful turning point in my career. It was not. Nothing very spectacular resulted.

The 1956 season over, I was supposed to go to Detroit with the company and then return to New York to be married—the six-weeks waiting period was up! It must have been all the excitement: I got the worst case of laryngitis I have ever had and I never made it to Detroit.

On November 17, 1956, Peter and I were married in a civil ceremony. The ceremony, conducted by State Supreme Court Justice James McNally, a friend of Miss Liebling's, took place in her apartment studio with Peter and me taking our vows standing in that same little circular design on her Oriental carpet where I had first sung for her when I was seven. It was a terribly stormy day. My side of the family was represented by my mother, my two brothers, their two very pregnant wives, and my Uncle Sydney, my father's baby brother and my favorite uncle. On Peter's side were his father and stepmother and his sister and brother. The only "outsiders" were Sue Yager, my oldest friend, who had been one of the Liebling Singers, and Désiré Defrère. My wedding gown had been made by my mother, as was my entire trousseau.

I had not met my father-in-law until that day. He had felt that the proper time to meet was when everything was signed, sealed and delivered. We hit it off right away. He put his arm around me and said, "I'm glad you're pretty at least. Call me Dad." He was a great old man with a fine sense of humor, and he was fiercely protective of every member of his family. At the wedding breakfast, in the Cottage Room of the Hampshire House, I asked him, "Well, Dad, what was your reaction when Peter told you he was going to marry a Jewish opera singer?" He looked at me, eyes twinkling, and replied, "Well, I'll tell you, dear. Peter and I were off Martha's Vineyard at the time, fishing in my boat, and I had two choices—I could throw myself overboard or I could go on fishing. Being the intelligent man that I am, I went right on fishing and said to Peter, 'Tell me about her.' "

Peter and I honeymooned in Nassau in a rented house. So that I could go fishing with Peter, my mother had made me a most stylish fishing ensemble —matching hat, jacket, and pants to wear with sneakers. The only trouble was that I got seasick while our boat was still tied to the pier. Peter must have had a lot of second thoughts about his new bride, who had laryngitis and was seasick most of the time. The laryngitis lasted for months and Peter maintains that it was the quietest period he has ever spent with me. I claim that he's the one who made me speechless.

When we returned from the honeymoon and drove up the driveway to our house in Cleveland, there pasted on the front door was a huge sign Lindley and Nancy had made. It said: WELCOME HOME, MAMA AND DADDY!

My first proposition from my husband-to-be, Peter Greenough,
written on a book of matches. 912 was my hotel room.

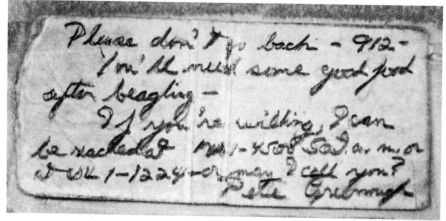

At the Cleveland Music Carnival, in August 1956, I sang my first Carmen. At right, I'm surrounded backstage by the men in my opera life: on my right is Norman Treigle, the toreador; on my left, Lloyd Thomas Leech, Don José. Below, Carmen takes a breather during rehearsal.

75

A last-minute substitute for Vivian Della Chiesa, I sing the role of Fiora in Montemezzi's The Love of Three Kings, *in Maestro Bamboschek's production at the Philadelphia Opera. With me is Frank Guarrera, singing the role of Manfredo, my husband.*

Relaxing with Lenny Bernstein during rehearsals for the concert version of Der Rosenkavalier *he conducted in 1956. I wanted to sing the Marschallin role; he said Sophie. Sophie it was and he was right.*

*In the New York City Opera production (above) of
Mozart's L'Impresario, in 1956, I, as Madame
Goldentrill (second from right), give what-for to my
rival, Madame Silverpeal (extreme left).*

*As Philine in Thomas's Mignon at the New York
City Opera in 1956. The costume I'm wearing showed
up on a chorus girl in a 1969 production of Mignon
with my name still sewn on it.*

At our first home, in Cleveland,
Peter and I with two of his daughters—
Lindley (at left) and Nancy.

Mr. and Mrs. Peter B. Greenough, after our wedding at Miss Liebling's studio.

En route to Nassau for our honeymoon Peter and I checked in at the airline ticket counter. This picture was published in the Nassau newspaper with a caption that read: "Newspaper editor Peter Greenough with his wife, Jackie Searles." Jackie Searles was a male comedian. Peter was upset.

7

"Miss Sills,
you are Baby Doe"

Alias Baby Doe

My two little stepdaughters must have thought that strange woman their father had married was really a traveling salesman, I was on the road so much of that first year of my marriage. Three weeks after the honeymoon I was in Texas for a three-city concert tour (including a place called Palestine, Texas, which Texans pronounce Palest*een* but I always called Palest*ine* to make myself feel more at home) and then on to Miami for a concert with the Miami Symphony Orchestra. It was difficult to explain to my husband, and indeed to myself, why I went on these trips, because, after expenses, I would probably come home owing somebody ten dollars. But at that stage of my career I had signed up for concerts a year in advance.

I did get home for Christmas and it was lovely. My mother came out from New York—a perfect grandma to the girls, laden with goodies, and always teaching them to make things with their hands. At that time I was completely useless in the kitchen: my mother had never taught me any culinary accomplishments, and when Peter and I were married we had a cook and other help in the house. Peter himself is a graduate of the Cordon Bleu and on special holidays he likes to do all the cooking. When he knew his mother-in-law was coming, he turned out Oysters Rockefeller, turkey stuffed with chestnut dressing and truffles, and Cherries Jubilee. All I did was set the table. After dinner my mother turned to me and said, "The dinner was just delicious. I knew you could do it if you set your mind to it." "Oh, Mama, *I* didn't cook any of this." "Well, did your cook make it?" "No, Mama, Peter did it, Peter did it all." She looked at me and said severely, "In *my* house your father never even knew the color the kitchen was painted." Later she gave me a long lecture: if you can read, she said, you can cook, so get cracking. Eventually Peter taught me to cook; I could turn out a fancy Hollandaise sauce before I knew how to boil an egg.

After Christmas I had to hit the road again. A concert in Jamestown, New York, so cold that only a hundred people showed up, and then on to another concert in Athol, Massachusetts. The best thing to be said about that junket was that I got to spend a weekend at my father-in-law's farm in Concord, in a farmhouse whose *newest* part dated to 1710. The farm, about three hundred and fifty acres, nineteen miles from the center of Boston, was a real gentleman's farm, the kind where the price of milk and the price of champagne are the same. My father-in-law's chauffeur, James, drove me to Athol in a limousine that was longer than the hotel's entrance. There I met my accompanist, Armen Boyajian. It was twenty degrees below zero. The concert took place in the school auditorium, and while the crowd assembled Armen and I waited in a classroom, he with his fingers in warm water and I vocalizing with steam gushing out of my mouth. The "crowd" was thirty people. I began to wonder what this career of mine was all about and why I was not at home with my nice, warm, handsome husband. I was even more depressed at what was facing me—something called a Johann Strauss Tour, which would keep me away from home for almost two solid months. Peter joined me as often as he could on that tour. Once he met me in Tampa, a convention town so overbooked that we had to stay in a "hot-pillow" joint: all night long sailors and their dates kept checking in and out of the "hotel" at very short intervals.

By then I had made up my mind to have a baby as soon as possible, but as that involves two people being in the same place at the same time, I was less than successful. Instead, that year I sang with the Memphis Symphony and the Jacksonville Symphony. I sang at the Brevard (North Carolina) Music Festival. I sang on the Woolworth Hour with Percy Faith's orchestra. I sang my first and only Gilda in a concert performance of *Rigoletto* in Chicago, conducted by Julius Rudel. My career was not exactly skyrocketing, but the reviews were all lovely and despite the long absences from home and family, my marriage was increasingly happy. I was having a marvelous time just learning to be Mrs. Peter Greenough.

That summer of 1957 I appeared again at Cleveland's Music Carnival, this time in a modern-dress, updated version of *Tosca*. By weird coincidence, at exactly the same time in Buenos Aires a young stage director named Tito Capobianco was also doing a modern version of *Tosca* at the Teatro Colón. Both productions were written up in *Time*. I had never heard of him before and he obviously had never heard of me. Later our careers were to mesh, with great consequences for both of us.

In the Cleveland *Tosca* there was one very colorful scene. In the second act, I, as Tosca, pick up a knife and stab the wicked Scarpia. He, played by William Chapman, had a small celluloid capsule between his fingers which he was supposed to slap across his white shirtfront to simulate blood when I "stabbed" him. Unfortunately, he held the capsule upside down, so that when he slammed it against his chest it squirted all over my face, my hair, my teeth; it must have held a gallon of thick, red "blood." The audience started to giggle and Bill, lying on the stage, was shaking with laughter. I had worked very hard to build up and sustain the tension that would climax in the actual stabbing and I was damned if I was going to let it all evaporate in giggles. So I kicked Bill—that stopped his laughter *and* the audience's.

We finished the act without incident but we needed a half-hour intermission to get me cleaned up for Act III.

Meanwhile, back at the New York City Center things had changed. Dr. Rosenstock had left, to be replaced for one year by Erich Leinsdorf. The company was in serious financial trouble. I went to the Yale Club with Cornell MacNeil, Norman Treigle, and Michael Pollack to beseech Newbold Morris to help save the company. He and a great many other people did come to the rescue and Julius Rudel was named artistic director. The eventual greatness of the New York City Opera dates from his arrival on the scene; Julius, in addition to being one of the world's finest conductors, is an administrative genius.

The 1958 spring season of the City Opera, Julius announced, would be devoted to contemporary American operas, sponsored by the Ford Foundation, the first season of its kind in New York City. The showpiece opera was to be *The Ballad of Baby Doe*, by Douglas Moore, which had been given its première in the mid-50s in Central City, Colorado. The rumor was all over New York music circles that Moore, Rudel, and Emerson Buckley, who was to conduct the opera, had auditioned scores of women singers for the role of Baby Doe but none had met with the approval of all three men. Nobody had asked *me* to audition; I had heard that whenever my name was brought up, the general reaction had been that I was simply too large for the role.

The New York première was scheduled for April 3. Walter Cassel was set for the role of Horace Tabor and Martha Lipton for Augusta, but by January 1 there was still no Baby Doe. One day Julius called me in Cleveland: how about auditioning? I'm not interested, I said. If Moore and Buckley have this preconceived notion that I'm too tall, there's no point in my auditioning just to be turned down. "Bubbela," Julius said soothingly, "let me at least send you some of the music, see what you think of it." He sent me the Willow Song and the final aria, both of which I loved immediately. I phoned Julius: Of course they're ideal for my *voice* but obviously the role is not ideal for me.

I was being very defensive at that point because I was irritated at being told that I was too large for something. I was simply not going to New York to be turned down. Then Emerson Buckley called me: Come on, come on in and audition. Buck, I said, there's no point if you think I'm too big for it. I won't be any smaller when I get to New York. "Get in here and sing," he said. Actually, he said something more vulgar than that.

I went to New York February 6, Peter's birthday, rationalizing my decision to audition by saying we were coming anyway to celebrate his birthday and see some shows. For the audition I wore the highest-heeled pair of new shoes I could find at Bergdorf's and a white mink hat of my mother's—I must have looked nine foot three. "Mr. Moore," I said to the composer, "this is how tall I am before I begin to sing for you and I'm going to be just as tall when I'm finished. We could save your time and my energy if you'd tell me now that I'm too big to play Baby Doe."

Douglas was such a dear sweet man, such a perfect gentleman, that I think he was thoroughly taken aback. He walked down the aisle to the stage and in a gentle voice said: "Why, Miss Sills, you look just perfect to me." I sang The Willow Song. Douglas walked down to the stage again. "Miss Sills," he said, "you *are* Baby Doe."

I loved the role. I read everything that had ever been written about her. I copied her hairdos from whatever photographs I could find. I absorbed her so completely in those five weeks of studying the opera that I knew her inside and out. I *was* Baby Doe.

At every performance Walter Cassel, as Horace, made me cry. When Horace was dying he would look up at me and sing "You were always the real thing, Baby" and I would sing, in reply, "Hush, close your eyes. Rest." Then I would take him in my arms and bawl like a baby. It was difficult to do the final aria after that scene. Walter and I lived those roles when we were on stage; there was never a moment during the performances when I didn't believe he was Horace Tabor. And even offstage he never called me Beverly or anything else, just "Baby."

The morning after opening night I grabbed the *New York Herald Tribune* from Peter before he had a chance to look at it. But there was no review on the regular review page. "Look at that," I said to Peter, "they didn't even cover it, can you imagine?" "Well," Peter said, "do you mind if I read the rest of the paper?" He turned to the front page and there—on the front page!—was the review.

The Ballad of Baby Doe is one of the great contemporary American works and should, I think, be a permanent fixture in the opera repertoire. I will always be grateful to Douglas Moore for having written it and for the opportunity it gave me to play opposite someone like Walter Cassel. Baby became an integral part of my operatic experience; it was difficult to shake her off even after I left the opera house. If I have ever achieved definitive performances during my career thus far, Baby Doe is one of them. The other three would be Manon, Cleopatra in *Julius Caesar*, and Queen Elizabeth in *Roberto Devereux*. They have been the only times in my entire career when I have walked out of the theater feeling that I have done everything I wanted to do with a role and that nobody else could have done it better.

In the New York City Opera fall 1957 season I
was given two new roles. One was Violetta in
La Traviata, *with baritone Igor Gorin singing
Germont. Good reviews but no handstands.*

*Walter Cassel as Horace and I as Baby Doe
locked in joyful embrace in Douglas Moore's
opera at the City Opera in 1958.*

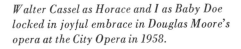

My other new opera in the City Opera fall 1957
season—The Merry Widow. My second-act
costume here was certainly put to good use. I
wore it for the first time as Micaela on the
Wagner tour in 1952. Later I wore it as
Carmen at the Cleveland Music Carnival in
1956. Here it is the third time around.

The up-to-date version of Tosca I sang at the
Cleveland Music Carnival in June 1957.
Scarpia, played by Bill Chapman, is wearing
a uniform strongly reminiscent of that of a
Nazi storm trooper.

87

8

Tragedy at home—
Not why me? *Why* them?

Peter and I decided that it was time to have a baby. I was six months
pregnant when I appeared at the New York City Opera in April 1959 to play
the character of The Prima Donna in the world première of Hugo Weisgall's
Six Characters in Search of an Author, based on the Pirandello play. The
opera was rather interesting and a personal success for me but it was not very
well received.

The real hero of the production may have been Edgar Joseph, head of
the City Opera's costume department, for the imaginative lengths he went to
conceal my pregnancy. He redesigned a copy of a Dior dress I owned,
gathered it high in front, and draped me in an enormous mink cape that
Peter had bought me or in large stoles or shawls. I was never allowed on
stage without a prop—usually a hatbox or an umbrella. One night the stage
director, William Ball, had the brilliant idea of my entering carrying a tiny
French poodle; it would not only effectively cover my tummy but would also
be the kind of item my character would normally own. On opening night, the

With my daughter Muffy at the Central City, Colorado, Music Festival, summer of 1959.

lady who lent us the poodle was very nervous that the poodle would be nervous, so she gave it a tranquilizer. As a result the dog looked dead, but at least, I thought, he'll be quiet. Suddenly, during one of my arias, I felt a warm trickle down the front of my dress; the dog, naturally, was peeing all over me. When I pulled him away from the dress, he woke up, startled, and howled at the top of his lungs throughout the whole aria, off-key. The audience was hysterical, and as far as I was concerned, *that* poodle's operatic career was finished. I never sang with a dog again.

Back home in Cleveland that summer, awaiting the birth of my baby, I got a call from Julius Rudel: Leopold Stokowski is opening our fall season with *Carmina Burana* and it would be nice if you could be in it. I went to New York to audition for Mr. Stokowski. I was very pregnant and he asked me if I were practicing breathing exercises. With his accent, it sounded like "breeding" exercises, so I replied, Obviously I practice breeding exercises. It was an Abbott and Costello routine—he said "breathing" and I thought "breeding." He offered me a role in *Carmina Burana* provided my baby was born on schedule, by July 25. She was not and I was never able to take that job with Stokowski.

Meredith "Muffy" Greenough was born August 4, 1959, and I became an asterisk on the City Opera roster—"On leave of absence." Except for two one-night stands with the company in 1960, I was to remain an asterisk because of family responsibilities for more than two years. Staying home with my little girl was a source of great joy, as was the feeling of settling in in Cleveland. I now had three girls to take care of and a twenty-five-room house with servants to run; I even had monogrammed towels for the first time in my life—most of the towels in our New York apartment had borne the label "Beth-El Hospital" (my brother Sidney interned there).

The whole family spent that first summer at the Central City, Colorado, Music Festival—my stepdaughters, Muffy, Nurse, and I—and Peter would fly in for weekends. I had accepted a summer engagement from Emerson Buckley, the music director. *I* thought I had agreed to do Lucia; he thought I had agreed to do Aida. Aida it became, and I enjoyed it; I think that I probably was the first Aida to wear an Afro in the role, spraying black dye into my curly hair. Living in Central City was very much like a kibbutz: part of your fee for singing was housing and a food allowance. It turned out to be a wonderful summer and I sang a lot of Aidas.

That fall my husband announced that we were moving to Boston: he was leaving the *Cleveland Plain Dealer* to write a financial column for a Boston newspaper. We settled in a nineteen-room house in Milton, Massachusetts, about ten miles south of Boston, and decided to have a second child. In April of 1961, when I was seven months pregnant, the phone rang and a deep voice said: "This is Sarah Caldwell." I had never met Sarah but I knew, of course, who she was. Even though her opera company was still young, she had begun to put her personal stamp on every production she did. I had once attended a production of her *Traviata* and was fascinated by how much she did with so little; she literally did it all with sheets and things made out of paper, yet it all worked and was truly distinctive. I was very much impressed with her work.

Sarah was planning a production of *Die Fledermaus* with Arthur Fiedler conducting. Would I play Rosalinda? "I'd be delighted," I said. "When?" In a few weeks, with rehearsals beginning in a few days. Wonderful, I said, and we hung up. My husband, who had been listening to this, asked dryly: "What are you planning to wear?" "Oh, costumes," I said airily. Then I looked down and realized what a shape I was in. I called Sarah back and said, "Miss Caldwell, I'm terribly sorry but I can't do your *Fledermaus* because I'm pregnant." There was a pause and then: "Weren't you pregnant five minutes ago?"

Our son, Peter Jr. (Bucky), was born June 29, 1961, weighing nearly ten pounds. We were on Cloud Nine: he was the first boy to be born into the Greenough family in forty-seven years and we at last had someone to carry on the name. A month later we suffered a tremendous shock: we learned that our daughter Muffy, who was then twenty-three months old, was deaf. We had suspected that something might be wrong with her hearing when she was only nine months old, but the doctors had convinced me that I was just being a worried first-time mother. She was such a bright child that she deceived us all. She would spend happy hours with picture books and she seemed to understand what they were saying. One day she moved close to a hot stove and I grabbed her just in time, screaming HOT! HOT! HOT! She spent the rest of the day wandering around the house saying hot, hot to everyone, her face lit up with a smile. It was the first word she had ever spoken. That near-miss with the stove forced us to have Muffy's hearing tested; it took only nine minutes to determine that she had a profound loss of hearing. "This is the worst day of my life," I said to Peter. "At least," he said, "it's over."

But it was not: shortly after the discovery of Muffy's loss of hearing, we learned that Bucky was mentally retarded. When he was two months old we asked a baby photographer to take some pictures of him. The photographer, trying to get Bucky's attention, suddenly looked startled. "Hey, lady," he said. "There's something wrong with your son—I can't get him to look at the birdie." There is no way of describing my initial desolation.

The discovery of our children's problems seriously altered our lives. In order to make Muffy as verbally communicative as possible we enrolled her in the Sarah Fuller School, a special nursery school in Boston. The process of teaching a deaf child to read lips and to speak is a frustratingly difficult one. What pulled us all through was the unfailing cheerfulness of my baby girl. She never stopped smiling, never stopped laughing. Even the most tedious sessions never seemed to tire her. She, her teacher, Merl Sigel, and I would crawl on the floor together for hours trying to get her to blow out a candle so that she would know how to pronounce the "wh" sound. The first candle she blew out was probably the most triumphant moment of her life— and of mine. When she saw how excited it made me, she couldn't wait to return home so that she could show her father too; she kept bringing out all the candles in the house for me to light and for her to blow out. She was always so proud of her accomplishments in learning. She has had many since and I hope will have many, many more.

During that period Sarah Caldwell and I became great friends. She knew of Muffy's condition, of course; she came to the house for dinner many times and Muffy fell in love with her. In February 1962, Sarah and I did our first opera together—*Manon*. The cast included John Alexander and Norman Treigle and in the orchestra pit was the Boston Symphony Orchestra; that ain't chicken liver! It was an exquisite production—once more what Sarah Caldwell did on a shoestring was nothing short of a miracle—and the reviews were raves. More important, for me, was the audience reaction; I had not provoked such enthusiasm anywhere before. I realized how much I needed opera now as a kind of refuge from personal problems.

Not that I felt much like singing, and especially if it meant going to New York and being separated from Muffy and Bucky. When I told Julius Rudel about the new developments in my life, he began to write me funny little "Dear Bubbela" letters signed "Julius Darlink" to get me to return to the City Opera. Once he phoned: "Listen, I have this marvelous Russian opera for you, *Boris Godunov*. You know how much I love you: you can play either Boris or Godunov." When I continued to resist, Julius turned stern: he insisted that I return to New York to sing Baby Doe in April—I owed it to him, he said: I had a contract to fulfill and he could no longer keep me on leave of absence status. Besides, he added, I was behaving foolishly.

I did sing that one performance of Baby Doe and then told Julius, That's it, I can't sing any more, I have too many other things on my mind.

The next month, on my thirty-third birthday, Peter gave me fifty-two round-trip tickets on the Boston–New York shuttle: I was to go to New York once a week, have my singing lesson with Miss Liebling, and see my mother. It was the best present he could have given me and he knew it; it was the kind of therapy necessary to force me out of the house and make me begin thinking about something besides family problems. Julius Rudel helped, too. He wrote me an order that fall on official stationery. He was tired of my excuses for not returning to work, I was to come to New York and sing and that was the end of it. He had a new opera for me to do—*Wings of the Dove*, by Douglas Moore, composer of *The Ballad of Baby Doe*—and he had also scheduled me to do *Louise*, with John Alexander as my lover and Norman Treigle as my father. I obeyed Julius.

Douglas had had me in mind when he began composing *Wings of the Dove*, but when I became pregnant with my son, he changed the role. The opera proved to be less successful than *Baby Doe*. But the *Louise* I sang on October 31, 1962, was one of those performances I will never forget. The *New York Times* the next day said it was "bland"; the *New York Times* didn't know what it was talking about. Alexander never sang better in his life, and Treigle and I gave the first of many performances together that made us walk out of the theater so moved that we were unable to speak. In the final act of the opera, when Louise decides to forsake her father for her lover, Treigle, caught up in the father's role, got so furious with me that he picked up a chair and threw it at me. I ducked (the chair hit the scenery) and then ran off the stage with Treigle sobbing out after me at the top of his voice: "Louise, Louise." When it was over, we were both crying. Jean Morel, the conductor, put his arms around us both, kissed us, and we three walked out on stage to take our bows, bawling our heads off. Bland performance—bull!

That night, in his hotel room, Norman wrote me a "Dear Bev" love letter: ". . . Watching you and hearing you just now in the aria and duet filled me with such beauty, admiration and emotion that I could hardly stand it. There are only a few people who have ever made me feel this way on stage and you are one who is on top of them all. . ."

Norman and I did our first *Faust* early the following year for Sarah Caldwell in Boston, at my suggestion. Sarah ran out of money before all the sets could be completed and we had to do the prison scene on a bare stage, but I never felt the need for scenery less. The starkness of that stage, Treigle in those black leotards as Mephistopheles looming ominously over my Marguerite—I felt for the first time that I had to fight for my stage life. Norman was always a great challenge to me; I like to think we brought out the operatic best in each other. Certainly we were never as inventive alone as we were on stage together and I never enjoyed operas as much as those in which we appeared together. It is a great credit to the City Opera that they recognized his talent and a great loss to the Metropolitan that it never put him on its stage. That voice, that temperament, that acting talent should have graced every opera stage in the world.

At about that time I was asked by Leopold Stokowski, who had never forgotten our pregnant audition, to sing four arias in a performance of Bach's *St. Matthew Passion* that he was to do with the American Symphony Orchestra in Carnegie Hall. I accepted but wrote him that I resented a cut he was making in one of my arias. He wrote back: ". . . From your delightful letter I fear you are not satisfied with these four inspired pieces of music by Bach. When I meet him in heaven, I will tell him about your 'frustration' and I am sure he will be deeply sorry, because he is such a nice man (although a genius). I hope you will pardon him and me." (Signed) "Always with friendly thoughts." I pardon him and Bach—wherever they are.

I was now only thirty-four, but a very mature thirty-four. In a strange way, my children had brought me an inner peace. The first question I had asked when I learned of their tragedies was a self-pitying "Why *me?*" Then gradually it changed to a much more important "Why *them?*" Despite their handicaps they were showing enormous strength in continuing to live as normal and constructive lives as possible. How could Peter and I show any less strength? After all that had happened, I felt that we could survive anything.

9

*All an "iron lung" needs
is comfortable shoes*

*As Olympia, the mechanical doll,
in* The Tales of Hoffmann.

My career seemed to be moving along at a faster clip; at least my fees were higher! And I was "singing around" quite a bit—at the Philharmonic opening of the 1963 Promenade Concert Series with André Kostelanetz; at Lewisohn Stadium, a Musetta in *La Bohème;* at Robin Hood Dell, a *Merry Widow* with Franz Allers; on to Honolulu with André Kostelanetz for a musical Viennese Night. Then in the fall back to the New York City Opera.

I sang *La Traviata* that season. I cannot say that the public suddenly felt they had discovered a new star, but I *can* say that people had begun to pay attention when I sang. The conductor was Franco Patane. He was very concerned with the musical values of an opera but didn't seem to care particularly about how it was staged or what was happening dramatically, probably because he was accustomed to opera in Italy, where the singers plant their feet and stare straight at the conductor.

Because I had a character to portray, I never looked directly at him although he was always in the periphery of my vision. After that opening night performance, Patane congratulated me on the fastest and cleanest coloratura that he had ever heard. Then he complained that I never looked at him when he was conducting. "I never look at you," I said, "but I always *see* you, Maestro." "I don't believe it," he said. During the second perform- ance of *Traviata,* when we came to the *"Sempre Libera"* aria, Patane began the tempo like a bat out of hell. I had never heard it played that fast before; I whirled around to look at him and on his face was a triumphant smile: he had forced Beverly to stare at him. And I dared not stop staring because the tempo was so unbelievably fast. I had not planned to sing the aria that way but it did make for a pyrotechnical virtuoso display that the audience loved. After that, whenever we got to the *"Sempre Libera,"* Patane and I had a joke going: I would whirl around and stare hard at him until he set the tempo. Then I would go about my stage business. "I can sing it," I once told him, "as fast as you can conduct it."

On the winter tour of the company that year I had the chance to sing my first Donna Anna in *Don Giovanni,* a role I had coveted and now con- sider one of my best. Julius Rudel and I have always had a special, unspoken understanding—no extravagant compliments, please. We always knew when a performance had that special quality; the look on our faces during and after a performance was enough to tell us how pleased we were with the way things had gone. But on that tour, after my first Donna Anna, when Julius came on stage to take bows with me, he blurted out, "My God, you sang like a goddess tonight!" I was so unprepared for that kind of hyperbole from Julius that I didn't even thank him; I just looked at him and said, "Yeah!" To this day, whenever we talk about my singing Donna Anna again, I always kid him. "How can I go back to singing her again? I can't sing it any better than a goddess. I should quit while I'm ahead."

On December 9, 1963, the New York City Opera celebrated its twen- tieth anniversary. I sang the Willow Song from *The Ballad of Baby Doe* at the celebration, then caught the flu and canceled a performance for the first time in my career. I have been nicknamed "The Iron Lung" because of my attitude that even if I had to be carried on stage feet first, I should sing a scheduled performance. It always devastates me to know that someone else is up there in *my* place. Thus when I cancel I am very, very sick. I figure that, even functioning a little bit less than at full potential, I still deliver a first-class performance—and I try very hard to do that.

I had recovered enough in the next few weeks to sing, in January of 1964, in Boston, my first Queen of the Night in Mozart's *The Magic Flute*. I wish it had been my last, and if I had a brain in my head it would have been. No role—not even Micaela—has ever bored me more. No role has given me less anticipation or less feeling of involvement; at one performance Peter and I backstage managed to address 250 Christmas cards between my first and second act arias! The role consists of five high Fs. If all five come out beautifully, you're a fabulous hit; if not, forget it, even though you may have sung all the rest of the aria beautifully. The only perfect performance I ever gave, by my own standards, was a Queen of the Night I did at the Tanglewood Music Festival conducted by Erich Leinsdorf. When I walked on stage to do the arias, Erich had a look in his eye that said, Don't-you-dare-miss-one-of-those-high-Fs. I didn't, by God, and because the performance was broadcast I know that there is a historic record attesting to my one perfect Queen of the Night.

Actually, I think my average for the role was four out of five high Fs, which I consider damned good. I know women who have made careers out of that Queen who had a worse batting average.

In February, for my debut with the New Orleans Opera, I sang for the first time all the lead female roles in *The Tales of Hoffmann* with Norman Treigle. It was the first of many *Hoffmanns* we were to do together and I think it was our greatest collaboration, vocally and histrionically. The concepts we created in the roles as we went along were totally original, more imaginative than anything else we had ever done together. In March I sang my first and only Adina in Donizetti's *The Elixir of Love* with Sarah Caldwell's Boston Company. Glynn Ross, who heads the Seattle Opera Company, had advised me against singing Adina because he considered the opera strictly a tenor's opera. I bet him five dollars that I could turn it into a soprano's opera; I won and he paid off. In April I sang with the Fort Lauderdale Symphony Orchestra, Emerson Buckley conducting, and a critic for the *Miami Herald* called me a "red-haired tomato." Other music critics around the country were also beginning to notice me. When I returned to New York in the fall to sing Donna Anna there for the first time, as well as Constanza in Mozart's *The Abduction from the Seraglio*, Winthrop Sargeant, the *New Yorker*'s music critic and one of the most respected in the country, called me THE *prima donna* of the New York City Opera. He was the first to bestow that title on me and I loved it.

The year ended on the road—a Marguerite in East Lansing, Michigan, a double-header in Chicago (*Die Fledermaus* in the afternoon, *The Merry Widow* in the evening); and a debut with the San Antonio Opera in Howard Hanson's *Merry Mount*, in which the first line I had to sing was, "Unhand her, you dastard."

That whole year reminded me of a story about Birgit Nilsson, the great Wagnerian soprano. In *Tristan and Isolde* she is on stage for most of the opera's four hours. After one of her usual magnificent performances, another soprano visited her backstage and said, "Really, Birgit, it's not so difficult, I don't understand why everybody makes such a fuss over it." "You're absolutely right," Birgit replied, "all you need is a comfortable pair of shoes." By the end of the year I felt the same way: it had been a good, busy year, my throat was in fine shape but my feet hurt terribly.

The year 1965 began on an unpleasant note. Sarah Caldwell and her Boston Company were doing the American première of an opera entitled *Intolleranza* and Sarah asked me to sing in it. The opera was written by Luigi Nono, son-in-law of the composer Arnold Schönberg. Mr. Nono is a very talented man but he has an unpleasant disposition. He is a member of the Italian Communist Party, or was at the time; perhaps he has since come to his senses. He came to Boston dressed in overalls and a worker's cap but he stayed in one of the city's most luxurious hotels (with the bill, I understand, being picked up by the opera company).

From the start of the production he raised havoc. The English translation of his opera, he complained, had lost all its poetry. The production itself was multimedia—huge slides were projected on a screen behind the performers, depicting man's inhumanity to man. Mr. Nono felt that man's inhumanity existed only in the United States. He had chosen slides of black men being lynched, for example, but refused to allow any of the Russian invasion of Hungary. At one point in the opera I had an aria entitled "Ban the Bomb," which contained a phrase "the screaming voices of Hiroshima," On the "shi" in "Hiroshima" I had to hit a high C-sharp. I tried to explain to Mr. Nono that on a note that high the text would be indecipherable and so it would be better to sing the word "Hiroshima" on a lower note so that people could understand. "No," he said, he wanted the high C-sharp to sound like the screaming of the bomb itself. When I said that I did not think I could bring it off, he began to yell, accusing me of acting this way because I did not want to admit my country's guilt in dropping the bomb.

The conductor was Bruno Maderna, who had a genius for difficult modern music. He was in total sympathy with the singers who had worked so hard to learn the music, and we all agreed to protest Mr. Nono's one-sided slide projections of man's inhumanity; they didn't *all* have to bear a made-in-America label. After a tremendous struggle we wound up with a kind of sixty-forty breakdown in the choice of slides as between the United States and the rest of the world.

On opening night there was one picket from the Polish Freedom Fighters outside the theater, protesting the very idea of Mr. Nono's opera being performed. Even the picket got bored and left at the end of the first act. In all fairness, Mr. Nono had written some intriguing music in the twelve-tone idiom, but most credit should be given to Sarah Caldwell and the cast of American singers who stuck it out for what, we felt, was as fine a performance of his opera as Mr. Nono could ever hope to have. Mr. Nono thought differently. He complained later that the reason his opera had not been a huge success in Boston was because the orchestra couldn't play the music—it was the Boston Symphony in the pit!—and in a letter to a newspaper he denounced the whole performance. I shall never sing another note of Nono's music—ever.

Another less than notable event in 1965 was my appearance as Mimi in the Seattle Opera's production of *La Bohème*. For me, Mimi has always looked exactly like Licia Albanese or Lucrezia Bori. I have always prided myself on knowing, or thinking I know, exactly what I look like on the stage; not even in the wildest leap of my imagination could I ever see myself looking like Mimi. I simply never got the hang of her. I love her, I cry when I see her performed. I also give thanks that I don't have to sing her anymore. I still look at the score from time to time, trying to figure out what eludes me about the character. Maybe it's because she is really a French heroine lost in the *verismo* of Italian opera; if she is supposed to be an Italian heroine, what's she doing in a French garret? The problem is mine alone, of course, because a great many famous sopranos have sung Mimi very successfully. But I was only too happy when, after my third performance of Mimi in Seattle, she was dead forever for me; not even mouth-to-mouth resuscitation could bring her back after that last dying gasp. I feel the same about Musetta in *La Bohème*, which I have sung only a few more reluctant times than Mimi. Musetta is a royal pain in the A. When I put Mimi, Musetta, Micaela, and the Queen of the Night to bed forever in my repertoire, they well deserved the rest.

Marguerite in *Faust* is something else. That year, when I sang the role for the first time in New York with Norman Treigle as Mephistopheles, the reviews were so overwhelming that Julius Rudel had them blown up and, for the first time in the company's history, displayed in the lobby of the City Center.

Norman and I were involved in another memorable performance that summer at—of all places—the Cincinnati Zoo Opera, so called because the theater had a roof but no sides and was smack in the middle of the zoo. (I remember a performance there, years later, of a *Traviata* which should have been billed "Starring Beverly Seals": throughout my entire "*Sempre Libera*" aria you could hear nothing but the barking of seals.) The Zoo Opera's artistic director was that same Tito Capobianco who had done the modern *Tosca* in Buenos Aires. Norman had met him in Mexico City. When Mr. Capobianco invited Norman to the zoo that summer of '65 to sing *The Tales of Hoffmann*, Norman agreed, but only if he could bring along his pal Beverly, with whom he had sung the opera before and who could sing all three soprano roles, so that Tito wouldn't have to hire any more sopranos, and so on. Tito was very intrigued and hired me sight unseen.

What Norman had neglected to tell him was that his pal Beverly stood five feet eight-and-a-half inches tall and weighed a hundred and fifty pounds. Tito had already decided that Olympia, the mechanical doll, should weigh in at about five feet and a hundred pounds, give or take a little—more or less like his wife, Elena (Gigi) Denda, who had been the prima ballerina at the Teatro Colón, in Buenos Aires. When I walked into rehearsal in Cincinnati, Tito's face fell; I figured that I had done something to upset him but inasmuch as I hadn't even said Hello yet, I couldn't imagine what it was. When I was introduced to Mrs. Capobianco, Gigi, she kept staring at me, and I thought something terrible must be happening. After the musical rehearsal I asked the Capobiancos what the trouble was. Gigi asked me what dress size I wore. I said, "Fourteen." Gigi said, "You see, we thought you were a Toddler Two." Our friendship dates from that first meeting: Gigi is my "sister" and Tito is my director.

The Cincinnati production of *The Tales of Hoffmann* was a sensation. The Petrouchka ballet originally planned for the doll in the first act was changed to take into account my size fourteen; the doll became a funny, Charlie-Chaplinesque walking doll with huge eyelashes that literally clicked when the eyes closed. Gigi did my makeup, and instead of painting on the red cheeks she cut out little circles of red masking tape and pasted them on my face. When we removed them after a performance, we would paste them on top of one of my pancake-makeup boxes. Unconsciously, we began to save all my "cheeks"; we did so many performances of *Hoffmann* that in a year every makeup box I opened had two little red masking tape cheeks pasted on it.

I got to show my legs on stage for the first time (other than that City Opera audition for Dr. Rosenstock) in *Hoffmann*. In the second act, as Giulietta, I was supposed to wear a long skirt with so many open slits that every time I moved the audience would get an unobstructed view of my legs. I balked at the costume at first; "I'm a singer," I complained, "not a strip teaser." But Tito convinced me I should wear the costume and, as usual, he was right: I got smash reviews for my voice *and* my legs.

Julius Rudel had agreed to do *Hoffmann* for Norman and me in New York at the City Center. But because there was no money for a new production, he was planning to use a mishmash of sets from four different operas. At the time Norman and I had agreed to the mishmash because we wanted so much to do our characterizations on stage, but when we realized that for a few thousand dollars we could bring the whole Cincinnati production to the City Opera Company, with Tito as director and Gigi doing the choreography, we began to badger Julius at every opportunity. One day when we were in Palo Alto to do a *Don Giovanni* with the City Opera, Norman came into my dressing room and said, "I want you to sing so that man on the podium (Julius) will just be sick to his stomach at the idea he can't give us the *Hoffmann* we want. Make him want to throw up in the orchestra pit." Julius was absolutely bowled over by our *Don Giovanni* that matinée; at the first-act curtain call he was in tears. *Giovanni* is, I think, his favorite opera; he conducts it as if Mozart were whispering in his ear. When Norman and I came off stage, Julius said to us, "What are you two guys doing to me? I'm absolutely limp." So Norman said, "Okay, Julius, you want a second act to match or you want a lousy one?" Julius looked at him quizzically. Norman: "Do we get the *Hoffmann* or don't we?" Julius: "You've got the *Hoffmann*, you've got the *Hoffmann*. Now leave me alone and finish this opera the way you started it."

Julius kept his word: he raised the money and brought *Hoffmann* to New York with the Capobiancos, who became permanent members of the company. Tito had separate triumphs of his own, of course, but he staged *all* of mine: *The Tales of Hoffmann, Julius Caesar, Manon, Roberto Devereux,*

Maria Stuarda, Anna Bolena, I Puritani. I work with the Capobiancos better than with any other director and assistant. They have studied every gesture I make, every reaction; they know how to deal with me when I am having difficulty with a character and how to leave me alone when I think I have caught on immediately. Gigi does my makeup and is always backstage with me before a première. She is an extremely calming influence. She knows what places in the opera are bothering me, and while she is putting on my makeup she will talk quietly about how we had decided to resolve the difficulties.

Tito has one of the most fertile minds in the business. He can think of fifteen different ways to do a scene until he finally finds the one that you are most happy with. If you are still unable to make up your mind at that point, he will decide for you. His taste is impeccable. I have total trust in anything Tito tells me to do and he, I think, feels the same about me. He likes to say I am a diamond that needs a magnificent setting and that he will always try to provide it for me. He always has.

As Giulietta in The Tales of Hoffmann, *1965.*

My first, and unfortunately not my last, Queen of the Night in Mozart's The Magic Flute—Boston, 1964. What a bore she is!

But Marguerite in Faust is something else. When I sang her for the first time at the New York City Opera (below, left) in 1965, the reviews were so favorable that Julius Rudel broke house tradition and displayed them, blown up, in the lobby.

Constanza in Mozart's The Abduction from the Seraglio (below, right) was another new role I took on at the City Opera in 1965. I was now singing so many different key roles in the repertory that the New Yorker critic referred to me as the prima donna in the company.

A scene from the Boston Opera Company's 1965 production of Luigi Nono's opera, Intolleranza. He was a no-no! I'm singing twelve-tone music against a backdrop of smoke and other curses depicting man's inhumanity to man.

Donna Anna in Mozart's Don Giovanni is a role I had always coveted. This scene is from the City Opera's production in 1965, with Norman Treigle as Giovanni and Donald Gramm as Leporello.

A scene from Sarah Caldwell's 1965 Boston Opera production of The Abduction from the Seraglio *with me, Constanza, third from left. It was an exquisite production, with the Boston Symphony in the pit.*

My first of only three performances in my life of Mimi in La Bohème—*all in a production of the Seattle Opera Company in 1965. It wasn't Rodolfo's fault, here played by tenor Luciano Saldari. I simply never got the hang of Mimi and so I have never sung her again.*

107

Julius Rudel and I share a hot dog after some opening or other. We've been sharing for more than twenty years at the New York City Opera. He's my Chulyuss Darlink and I'm his Bubbela.

Gigi Capobianco and me—she's the Toddler Two.

Tito Capobianco and me. He's my director, and I'm his jewel who needs a perfect setting and gets it when he's around to create it.

10

If I don't get Cleopatra, I quit!

Cleopatra—the turning point of my career.

Early in 1966, the New York City Opera moved from the ancient City Center on West Fifty-fifth Street to its shiny, glamorous new home in the New York State Theatre, part of the Lincoln Center complex. The first season that spring, devoted to contemporary works (I did *Baby Doe* again), was not considered the official opening; that was scheduled for the fall, with the première to be Handel's *Julius Caesar*. Norman Treigle was to be Caesar and Julius Rudel had invited Phyllis Curtin to return to the City Opera (she had left its roster to join the Met) to sing Cleopatra.

Julius' decision to use Phyllis annoyed the hell out of me. There was nothing personal in it: Phyllis had been my friend for more than twenty years, still is, and as an artist she is without peer. But I felt that asking her back to do Cleopatra implied that no one in the City Opera company could sing the role and that just wasn't true—*I* could sing it. I had already sung several of the arias in my recitals and I felt that the role was ideal for me. Besides, as the *New Yorker* critic had written, I was now the *prima donna* in the company; my repertoire included key roles—Constanza in *The Abduc-*

tion from the Seraglio, all the roles in *The Tales of Hoffmann,* the Queen of the Night, Donna Anna—and it would be difficult to replace me in those roles. I decided to talk turkey with Julius: either I get the Cleopatra role or I resign from the company.

I discussed it first with John White, the extraordinary managing director of the company, and the pal to whom I give the final wave at all my curtain calls. He felt that I had a valid beef. Then at breakfast with Julius in his home I made my case: "If you gave Cleopatra to anyone else already with the company," I said, "I would not protest. But going outside the company to find another soprano was a public admission that nobody then in the house could sing the role. Well, how about me?" Julius said my arguments seemed reasonable. Then he looked at me mischievously and said, "You're not really going to resign from this company, you're too much a part of it and it's a part of you, just the way it is with me, and besides, you know how you love to come to New York." "True," I replied, "but I feel so strongly about this that if I don't get the Cleopatra, I *will* resign, and then I'll hire Carnegie Hall and sing five Cleopatra arias just to get her out of my system, because, by God, I'm going to sing Cleopatra in New York!"

Julius is an extremely fair man. To his everlasting credit, he said, "Yes, the part is yours." What arrangements he had to make with Phyllis I do not know. In any case, there has never been any bitterness between Phyllis and me over the matter.

That summer, while I was working on Cleopatra, I received my first offer from the Metropolitan Opera Company—to do a performance as Donna Anna at Lewisohn Stadium in New York with my old friend Dr. Rosenstock conducting. Robert Herman, Rudolf Bing's assistant manager, who tendered the offer, told me that everyone at the Met was very happy to have me finally make my debut with them. "To me," I replied, "a debut in an opera house takes place on the stage of that opera house, *not* in an open-air stadium." I would be delighted, I continued, to be a guest in the performance, but I would not consider it my debut at the Met nor consider myself a member of the Metropolitan Opera Company. I signed the contract, they paid my fee. Then

I was informed that the big Donna Anna aria, *"Non mi dir,"* in the second act was to be deleted. When I protested that I would not do the performance under those circumstances, the aria was restored. It was a show stopper. Mr. Bing did not attend the performance and it was another six years before the Met nibbled at me again.

By sheer coincidence, the Met had scheduled for the opening of its new Lincoln Center home in 1966 the world première of Samuel Barber's *Anthony and Cleopatra*. The Met's Bob Herman said to me at the time that the City Opera was foolish to open with *Julius Caesar* against the Met's *Anthony*. My answer was that inasmuch as Mr. Handel had got there first we had a perfect right to do *Caesar* on our opening night. And so it was a head-to-head competition. As it turned out, it was really no contest. Despite Barber's gorgeous music and the incredibly beautiful singing of Leontyne Price as Cleopatra, the Met opening, rumored to have cost three quarters of a million dollars, was a disaster—overproduced, overdirected, over-everything, a Hollywood extravaganza in which the opera got lost. Our opening, quite simply, was a complete triumph—a sixty-thousand-dollar authentic Handel, duplicating the way the opera had been performed in the composer's time. The women from the neck down were dressed in baroque gowns; from the neck up they wore headdresses that would suggest the character—Cleopatra in one scene, for example, wears a headdress with an asp in it. The men wore togas. Some people believe that in Handel's time singers used to make up their own ornamentation—the flowery vocal embellishments to a melody—on the spot during a performance. I do not believe it: it was a great period for show-offish singing, for trying to outdo one another, and the ornamentation must have had to be well-prepared and rehearsed in advance. In any case, we tried to stick with what we thought was authentic and tasteful Handelian ornamentation.

The cast was inspired and memorable. Norman Treigle as Julius Caesar looked and acted like John Gielgud in the role and sang like a Roman god. The rest—Beverly Wolff, Maureen Forrester, Dominic Cossa, Spiro Malas—were equally awesome. When the performance was over, I knew that some-

thing extraordinary had taken place. I knew that I had sung as I had never sung before and I needed no newspapers the next day to reassure me. Julius came to my dressing room and we shared what I think was the most intimate moment in our more than twenty-five-year friendship. He put his arms around me and said, "God takes care of people like me. I'm very lucky that I shared such an evening with you." Then he turned and walked out of the room.

Of all the nights in my performing life, including the night I made my debut at the Metropolitan nine years later, none will remain in my memory as long as that opening night of *Julius Caesar*. It was—and I don't mean to be immodest, but after all these years I *am* a pretty good judge of performances—one of the great performances of all time in any opera house. It was the kind of night when the audience was so caught up in the general euphoria that it never even noticed a bizarre piece of stage business. As Ptolemeo, Spiro Malas had a small band of soldiers—nonsinging, spear-carrying extras paid a couple of dollars per performance just to add physical presence to the staging. Their instructions were simple: when Mr. Malas goes on stage, follow him and stand behind him; when he exits, exit with him. On opening night, while on stage, Spiro suddenly could not remember the opening words of his next recitative. While someone else was singing an aria, he quietly and with great dignity marched off to the wings to consult the score. What he did not notice was that his soldiers were dutifully following him off stage and then back on. The audience apparently did not notice anything awry either. We in the cast thought it was hilarious: the two opening words that Spiro had forgotten were—"Julius Caesar."

Julius Rudel and I have talked often about reviving the opera, but you can't go home again. Without Norman Treigle around (he died in 1975) it no longer has much appeal for me and I doubt that I will ever sing it again. When you feel that you have done a definitive anything in your life, it's best to leave it at that.

The day after the première of *Julius Caesar* I flew home. There was an excellent review in the *New York Times*, but I didn't see any other reviews until I returned to New York four days later for my next performance. They were fabulous: all the critics, national and international, had been in New York for the opening of the Met, and as we were only a few hundred yards away across the plaza, it had been no great chore for them to come to our opening, too. There were five hundred fan letters in my mail box at the theatre; before, I used to average about ten a week.

Needless to say, *Julius Caesar* was the turning point of my career. But strangely enough, that success, when it came, meant less to me than it might have if it had occurred five years earlier. Let me try to explain. Once, during rehearsals for the opera, when I was singing for Julius, he said to me in awe, "Where the hell did you learn to sing like that?" An interesting question. My voice had not changed; *I* had. Now, instead of using my singing just to build a career, which is what I had been doing up to that time, I was singing for pure pleasure. I was singing not because I wanted to be Beverly Sills Superstar, but because I needed to sing—desperately. My voice poured out more easily because I was no longer singing for anyone's approval; I was beyond caring about the public's reaction, I just wanted to enjoy myself.

At the same time, as I indicated earlier, I had found a kind of serenity, a new maturity as a result of my childrens' problems. I didn't feel better or stronger than anyone else but it seemed no longer important whether everyone loved me or not—more important now was for me to love them. Feeling that way turns your whole life around: living becomes the act of giving. When I do a performance now, I still need and like the adulation of an audience, of course, but my *real* satisfaction comes from what I have given of myself, from the joyful act of singing itself.

This all may sound a little Pollyannaish and I don't consider myself a Pollyanna. But it is the only explanation I can give for the way I sang in *Julius Caesar* that night—and for the way the audience, sensing my own joy, responded.

114

Norman Treigle as Julius Caesar and I as Cleopatra.

11

Manon—
"Think Lolita, think Lolita"

Swinging away as Manon.

When our little boy Bucky was six, Peter and I had to face the sad realiza-
tion that he could no longer live at home with us. He was a beautiful big boy,
brown eyes, brown curly hair, a dead giveaway for his mother. But he was
autistic, could not speak, and was showing signs of epilepsy. I was against
sending him away to a special school but Peter and my mother convinced me
that he needed the teaching and the therapy that only a special institution
could provide; keeping him at home would deny him whatever help was
possible. We decided to put him in the same school in Massachusetts where
my stepdaughter Diana had been since 1959. At least we could visit them
regularly.

It was, of course, a particularly tense, highly emotional period for me
and I sought out Julius Rudel to find me some challenging, absorbing project
that would help me through it. We decided that I would sing *Il Trittico*,
Puccini's trilogy of one-act operas. No soprano in New York, to my knowl-

edge, had ever sung the leading roles in each of the three one-acters on the same night; I decided that would be my challenge.

The week my son was to leave home, I sang a scene from Strauss's *Daphne* in a concert with the Boston Symphony Orchestra conducted by Erich Leinsdorf. By that time Erich and I had become close friends, and of course he knew about Bucky. While the orchestra was playing a long orchestral interlude, I looked at Erich. He had tears in his eyes; so did I. When the performance was over, we took no curtain calls. Hand in hand, we walked off, he to his dressing room, I to mine. We did not speak. We felt, I think, that we were sharing a rare moment of intimacy. We have never talked about it but I know he remembers that moment as well as I do.

Il Trittico opened March 8, two days after my son had gone away to school. I don't remember much about my performance but it must have been memorable. *Suor Angelica,* one of the three operas, is the story of a young noblewoman who has become a nun in expiation of a scandal in her life—she is an unwed mother. In one scene the Sister (my role) is told that her son, whom she had been forced to abandon, had died two days earlier. I had considerable trouble getting through that scene, breaking down in tears several times. The conductor was Franco Patane, and many years later I learned from his son that Franco had also wept uncontrollably as he was conducting that scene. He too had difficulty finishing the opera. When *Suor Angelica* was over, I vowed that I would never sing her again, because of the painful associations it had for me, and I never have.

Singing all three roles in *Il Trittico* was purely a stunt; the roles are written for three different types of voices. One critic asked afterwards why I, with a voice like peaches, had to be every apple in the orchard. She was absolutely right, of course, and I will never repeat the stunt. But at the time it served its purpose: it certainly occupied my mind.

For the 1967 fall season of the New York City Opera, Julius Rudel was mounting a new production of Rimsky-Korsakov's *Le Coq d'Or*. Norman Treigle was to play King Dodon and I the Queen of Shemakha. The Capobiancos, who were to direct it, were very busy at the same time working on a new production of *Tosca,* and when we started rehearsals for *Le Coq* they were not paying any attention to me. Other people seemed to be moving around carrying palm leaves back and forth but I would just be standing there in the center with no stage business plotted. It was totally unlike the usual Capobianco operation and with only a week left before the première I finally complained to Gigi: "What am I supposed to *do* in this role? Why am I just standing still and where is my costume?" Gigi said, "We've been somewhat afraid to tell you but you have to dance throughout the entire role." "Dance!" I shrieked. "I barely can do social dancing. And what do I wear?" The Capobiancos produced what looked like three and a half veils. Those, together with a five-story, fragile, bejeweled crown like a French spun-sugar concoction, were to be my entire costume. Then Gigi, a former ballerina, demonstrated the dance I was to do—a thirty-five-minute belly number. I just stared at her. "Impossible," I said. "I can't wear this bikini with my belly button showing, I can't wear this flimsy bra, I can't dance. Out of the question." "Look," Gigi said soothingly, "I'll work with you, and if you still feel you can't do it, then we'll change it."

By the end of the first three hours of dance rehearsal I was bruised, battered and charley-horsed but you could not have taken that dance away from me for all the money in the world. I was into the belly-dancing bit literally up to my navel and I loved it. The dance also helped me define the role which up to that point had eluded me; I decided the best way to play Queenie was like Mae West, poking fun at her own sexiness. It was such a complete change of fare for Norman and me from *The Tales of Hoffmann* and *Julius Caesar* that we had a ball. So did the audience: the ticket lines around Lincoln Center fountain were the longest in the company's history. Even our version of the opera on television brought a huge rating. Bless the public's taste: it *was* a knockout of an opera.

After the success of *Julius Caesar,* Julius Rudel had called me into his office: "We're going to do *Coq d'Or* for Norman in 1967 and then, in 1968,

we'll do a special one for you. Start thinking about what you'd like it to be."
Manon, I said immediately, and just as quickly Julius said yes. He was as
excited about the project as I.

Our *Manon* was a Fragonard painting come to life—his famous painting
of the lady on the swing. Gigi bought me a whole new case of makeup for
the part—it was all pink, pink, pink. The sets alone created an atmosphere
that tore your heart out; Julius Rudel said that the second act apartment of
the Chevalier des Grieux reminded him of the small Paris hotel he had stayed
in as a young man after World War II. The tenor who sang Des Grieux was
Michael Molese, a young American who had done a lot of singing in Italy.
We used to fight terribly during rehearsals, not because Michael didn't
understand the role—he did—but because he was trying so hard to do it all
exactly right. I had considerable trouble with my own role at the start. You
look too innocent, Tito would say to me, Manon isn't that innocent. In the
bedroom scene in Act II, when Manon is reading the letter that Des Grieux is
about to send to his father explaining their love, one line goes: "Yesterday
she was sixteen." I burst out laughing during rehearsal and asked Tito,
"What the hell am I supposed to do with *that* line?" "Think Lolita, think
Lolita," he replied, and suddenly the whole character fell into place for me.

Everything in the production was perfect, but I remember especially the
scene in Act III that takes place in the Seminary of Saint Sulpice. Des Grieux
has gone there to become a priest and Manon tries to entice him out of that
decision. I was wearing a beautiful lace gown and carrying a chiffon scarf.
As I circle and circle Des Grieux, he suddenly seizes the scarf and buries his
head in it as though he can no longer hold out against my perfume. Every
night the public would go wild after that scene.

Whenever I was to sing Manon, I couldn't wait to get to the theater. I
would come in two hours early and spend a half-hour on Manon's swing,
swinging slowly back and forth. I think that was the real beginning of my
schizophrenic personality; I suddenly felt as I was walking into the theater
that I was no longer Beverly Sills but the lady I was about to portray. For

those three hours at least I was totally divorced from myself and my problems.

After *Julius Caesar,* offers began pouring in from all over the world. I was still the girl who couldn't say no, too excited at being invited to all those places every soprano dreams of. In a period of three weeks I sang on three different continents. Norman and I did a *Tales of Hoffmann* in Santiago, Chile, and a *Julius Caesar* in Buenos Aires. Tito Capobianco, for political reasons, was not allowed to accompany us to Argentina, which annoyed me and I made my unhappiness clear to the authorities. The conductor of that performance was Karl Richter, who never believed in cuts; as a result, I sang my last aria at 12:40 A.M. I went to Vienna to do three Queen of the Nights and three Violettas at the State Opera. Because of a badly infected ear I had to cancel all but the first Queen. It was rather unpleasant: the opera director threatened that if I canceled he would make such a *scandale* that I would never again be invited to sing in Europe. I was foolish enough at the time to believe him. I have been invited many times since to sing in Europe and even with the Vienna Opera—now under new management.

My second trip to Vienna was to do a record for ABC of Donizetti and Bellini arias. I had stalled ABC in 1967 when they first made the offer because I wanted to ask my friend Roger Hall, then head of artists and repertoire at RCA, if he was interested in my recording those arias for him. What street does your mother live on? Roger asked. Fifty-ninth Street, I said. Well, Roger said, it'll sell three records on Fifty-ninth Street and your mother will buy them all. Roger, I said, one day you're going to have to eat that record. I should have insisted on it—the recording has sold more than 100,000 copies.

Between engagements at the City Opera, in Europe, and in South America I was still taking my show on the road here. I did *Traviata*s in Cincinnati and Texas; *Hoffmann*s in Los Angeles and San Antonio; a *Faust* in Orlando. And I got to do my first *Lucia*—in Fort Worth, Texas. Somebody asked me how come I had never done a *Lucia* before. Because nobody asked me, I replied. When *Time* did a cover story on me in 1971, they called me "The Fastest Voice Alive." That was a reference to Thomas Schippers's statement that I could move my voice faster than anybody else alive. But it could also be applied to another of my strengths: I am a quick study. I can learn almost any part quickly and usually can be talked into going anywhere to sing it. Indeed, I was the work horse at the City Center ("Need someone to sing three nights in a row? Call on old Beverly.") and I was very proud of it. When I am gone, if my career is ever discussed, I hope it will be in terms of the kinds of performances I gave in repertory all those seasons at the City Opera. I'll settle for that.

"Bucky," Peter Greenough, Jr., at five.

When I learned that our son Bucky had to be
sent off to a special school in 1967, I decided
I needed something especially challenging to
help me during a difficult period. And so I
sang all three roles in Puccini's Il Trittico in
the same evening: Suor Angelica (top left),
with Frances Bible in the role of my aunt;
Giorgetta (top right) in Il Tabarro, with
Placido Domingo playing Luigi; and Lauretta
in Gianni Schicchi (right).

*At the San Francisco Opera production of the same opera in 1971, Tito Capobianco,
who directed both productions, gives me a helping hand during rehearsals.*

125

At Tanglewood in 1968 I sang a concert with Erich Leinsdorf conducting the Boston Symphony Orchestra. This was only a few days before my son Bucky was to leave home permanently for a special school and Erich knew it. When he began to conduct the orchestral interlude from Strauss' Daphne, we were both moist around the eyes.

"Chulyuss Darlink" Rudel and me laughing it up—as usual.

When it's apple-throwing time in San Francisco. The invisible target is Luciano Pavarotti, who had just pinched my behind during a rehearsal break.

127

Queens,
madwomen,
country girls,
army mascot
—I sing'em all

As Cleopatra in the New York City Opera's 1966 production of Handel's Julius Caesar.

My—and Donizetti's—three queens: Queen Elizabeth I (left) in Roberto Devereux, *which I consider my finest artistic achievemer* Maria Stuarda (below); *and* Anna Bolena (bottom left).

Opposite: Doing my belly number as Queen Shemakha in Rimsky-Korsakov's Le Coq d'Or.

Norman Treigle and me having a marvelous time in two scenes from Offenbach's The Tales of Hoffmann. *Above, he is Dr. Miracle, I Antonia, in Act III. Opposite: Norman as the evil Dapertutto and I as Giulietta in Act II.*

Admiring my jewels as Marguerite in Gounod's Faust.

Dying, as Manon, in the arms of my lover, Des Grieux (Placido Domingo).

Going mad as Lucia, while Raimondo the Chaplain (Robert Hale) stands by.

A scene from I Puritani *at the New York City Opera: Lord Arthur Talbot (played by Enrico di Guiseppe) kisses my (Elvira's) hand as a chorus of Puritans solemnly looks on. Arthur has just been given permission by my father to marry me, although he's on the other side in the battle between the followers of Cromwell and of the Stuarts.*

As Marie in Donizetti's The Daughter of the Regiment.

12

La Scala—
"Well, Bubbles,
now we've done it all"

Every career, when it begins to take off as mine did after *Julius Caesar*, needs a mentor—one person who will make decisions based not on personal gain but on an honest love for the individual whose career he is involved with. There are always a great many people ready to come backstage to tell you how wonderful you were when you really were not. There are also many people—thank God, not as many—ready to tear you apart after even your best performance. I have always felt that I was the person best qualified to judge my own performances. I have lived with my talent, such as it is, longer than anyone else. I know its capabilities and its limitations. I know when I have done a crackerjack job and when I have not. But it is still invaluable to have someone who can come backstage after a performance and render a completely sincere cold assessment of what you have done right or wrong —even if *he* is wrong!

I found my mentor in Edgar Vincent, who runs what is probably the most successful public relations firm for the classical performing arts in the country. Even before we knew each other Edgar had helped push my career: he was instrumental in introducing me to André Kostelanetz, and whenever Erich Leinsdorf, then musical director of the Boston Symphony, needed a soprano Edgar would always recommend me.

One day Edgar got a phone call from Thomas Schippers, the American conductor then living in Rome. Schippers was desperate: he was to conduct a new production of Rossini's *The Siege of Corinth* in April at La Scala to commemorate the centenary of Rossini's death, and his soprano, Renata Scotto, who was to sing the leading role of Pamira, would be too pregnant to perform. Did Edgar know *anyone* who was proficient in Italian, could learn a long, difficult role in four months, and could fly to Rome to spend some time learning the role with him? "Call Beverly Sills," Edgar said, and hung up.

And that is how I came to make my debut at La Scala. First I had to get out of several previous conflicting engagements. I phoned Julius Rudel: "By all means," he said, " so long as you're back at the City Opera for the opening of *Manon*." I phoned Erich Leinsdorf, with whom I was scheduled to do several concerts: "Go, you're released." I wrote to Eugene Ormandy (I didn't know him well enough at the time to phone): he wrote back a funny, tongue-in-cheek letter saying he could think of no reason in the world why I would consider La Scala more important than doing three performances of *Elijah* with him, but, of course, if that was the way I felt about it, fine.

At the beginning of February I flew to Rome to begin work on the score with Mr. Schippers. We had never met before—I doubt that he had even heard me sing. I was very nervous. In the score he had sent me was insert after insert because the version of the opera he was planning was a rough combination of three different Rossini operas—the original Italian version of the *Siege* and scissored-in excerpts from an earlier Rossini opera called *Maometto II* and from the rewritten version that Rossini had done for the *Siege*'s first successful performance in Paris in 1826. The vocal score was extremely complex. It had so many notes that I wish I had been paid by the note rather than by the performance.

At Tom's apartment, his wife Nonie, sensing how nervous I was, suggested a spot of tea. Great idea. While she was in the kitchen Tom explained to me that what I regarded as a hodgepodge of versions of several operas was actually the way the opera was performed in Rossini's time. When Nonie came back with a tray, she promptly tripped over the rug—tea, cookies, lemons, and Nonie went all over the room. She looked up. "How's *that* for making a nervous guest feel at home?" My nervousness had already gone. Everything seemed to jell between Tom and me once we started work. It turned out we were both bridge nuts. "Okay, fifteen-minute break," he would say during our first rehearsals, and then we would talk bridge. He was so enthusiastic about the opera, as was I, that we eagerly awaited the debut. *The Siege of Corinth* had last been performed at La Scala in 1852.

On March 8 I arrived in Milan and rented an apartment in a hotel. Marilyn Horne and her little girl were living in the same hotel, and when my mother, Peter, and Muffy came over to join me, we all became one big happy family. The street our hotel was on, we learned later, was famous for its colorful retinue of "ladies of the evening." Every night they would line up about a foot apart, heavily made up and dangling the inevitable enormous handbags. Muffy, who was ten, thought they were absolutely gorgeous; every evening as we passed the ladies on the way to the theater or to dinner, her eyes would pop. One day she asked me, "Mama, how do you say 'beautiful' in Italian?" "*Bella, bella*," I told her. The next night Muffy went up to one of the more colorful ladies, put a great smile on her face, and said, "*Bella, bella*." The woman was so touched that she reached into her handbag, pulled out a piece of chocolate, and gave it to Muffy. *Grazie.*

Marilyn Horne had already made her debut at La Scala, in *Oedipus Rex*. She knew her way around at the opera house and was a great help to me. She had already learned that at La Scala you don't say please, you always talk in loud, booming tones, and you play *prima donna* twenty-four hours a day. Otherwise nobody pays any attention to you. It took me a while to learn. One day the woman who was making the costumes came to me with a big tape measure, measured me, and then showed me the design of the costume intended for Madame Scotto. It was in gold and I felt that with my hair, silver would be much more suitable. Even though the original costume had already been cut and sewn, Nicola Benois, who designed both the sets and the costumes, agreed that silver was better and we both instructed the costume lady to redo the gown. *"Non si preoccupa, Signora,"* she said. "Don't worry about it." At the first dress rehearsal parade, a custom at La Scala, the ladies of the Costume Department marched across the stage holding up the costumes to spotlights to determine if there were any problems; there was my costume—still in gold. I reminded the lady—silver. *"Non si preoccupa,Signora."* On the day of the first piano dress rehearsal I walked into my dressing room and hanging on a hook was my costume—in gold. I took the costume, walked on stage, and asked the Technical Director to summon the costume lady. "Did I not tell you to make this costume in silver?" *Si, Signora.* "Did I not tell you four or five times to make this costume in silver?" *Oh, si, Signora.* I took the gold costume, folded it very carefully into a square, lifted a pair of scissors the costume lady had dangling around her neck, and slowly and deliberately I cut the costume in half. Then, with a smile, I said, "Now you go back upstairs and make the costume in silver."

The chorus broke into wild applause; they cheered as though I had just sung the most divine aria in the world. After the dress rehearsal I went upstairs to see Signor Luciano Chailly, who was then artistic director of La Scala. He smiled: "Well, we were all wondering when it was going to happen." "When what was going to happen?" "Well," he replied, "you're always so cheerful, you speak so softly, we kept wondering when is this lady who is so famous for her acting temperament, when are we going to see some of her temperament? Now we've seen it." "No," I said, "you haven't seen my temperament, you've just seen me temperamental. There's a big difference."

Marilyn Horne and I lived in excited anticipation of opening night of *The Siege of Corinth:* the opera suited us both vocally to a high C—of which we had plenty. I do not remember even being nervous, but Gigi Capobianco, who had accompanied me to Milan for the opening, says that I was—I forgot to wear my false eyelashes and played the whole opera without them. I don't think that any two female American singers performing together at La Scala ever equaled the success we had; the ovations were endless and I shall never forget them. Not that the public at La Scala is any more discerning than operagoers in the United States, who, I think, make up one of the most discriminating, intelligent audiences anywhere. But there is an undeniable unique mystique about singing at La Scala; the house has, after all, given world premières of, among other operas, *The Love of Three Kings, Andrea Chenier, La Gioconda, Madama Butterfly, Mefistofele, Otello, Turandot.* It is the historic "golden theater." I was very conscious of all the great singers who had appeared there before me; I was more than pleased to have joined their ranks. And I picked up three new names given me by the Milanese: La Sills, *La Fenomena* (which is self-evident), and "Il Mostro." The last title made me laugh: it means "The Incomparable One" but it can also mean "The Monster."

We gave six performances of the opera at La Scala. The production became known as The Siege of the Americans because the three leads and the conductor were all Americans—Marilyn, Justino Diaz, and I, and Tom Schippers. So triumphant was our reception by the Italian public that, probably for the first time in La Scala history, we even managed to beat the claque. The claque at La Scala is an evil, archaic bit of nonsense; with audiences as knowledgeable as they are today, I am amazed that all the great singers who have appeared there have not simply banded together and told the claque to go to hell. We had been warned by colleagues in the United States that the claque would make serious financial demands on all of us in view of the fact that we were Americans singing in *their* house. Sure enough, as soon as we arrived the head of the claque paid a visit to Maestro Schippers to make his pitch. Tom and the rest of us decided that the way to beat them was to join forces: each of us made a contribution of lira, put it all together in the same envelope, and handed it over as a group. It worked: it cost us each $25 for the entire run of the opera and after the opening night truimph the head of the claque knew that it was pointless to try to dun us again.

While we were still in Milan, *Newsweek* appeared with a cover story on me, pegged to the La Scala debut. During a five-day break between performances, when Peter and I were visiting Venice, a newspaper vendor, hawking the latest wares in the Piazza San Marco, recognized me from the picture on the *Newsweek* cover. Everywhere we went that afternoon the vendor followed, screaming at the top of his lungs, "Here's the woman on the cover of *Newsweek*, here's the woman." He peddled a lot of magazines and I made a lot of new friends; there were a great many Americans in the Piazza that day. It was my first experience with a phenomenon my husband has referred to many times since, my "recognition factor." I have, for example, Peter will say, a high recognition factor on the first floor of Bloomingdale's. That day in Venice he said, "You've certainly a high recognition factor in the Piazza San Marco."

On the plane returning home, Muffy, exhausted, was asleep across the aisle in Peter's lap. My mother and I were seated next to each other. "Well, Bubbles," she said, "now I feel we've done it all." That is exactly the way I felt.

In my dressing room at La Scala making up for my debut. On the table to my left is a small decorated egg that Miss Liebling, too ill to make the trip to Italy, gave me as a present.

Nervous? Who's nervous? In my hotel room in Milan I tootle away between rehearsals of
The Siege of Corinth.

Between performances at La Scala, Peter and I toured the countryside and, like all tourists, had our picture taken.

13

Lucia, or how to go mad all over the world

As a result of my La Scala success, and the *Newsweek* cover, I quickly received two more foreign assignments—one in the Philippines, the other in Naples, Italy. The sponsor of the six concerts I was booked to sing in the Philippines was Eugenio Lopez; he owned the Manila Electric Light Company as well as several newspapers and his brother was vice-president of the country.

I must say that Mr. Lopez and all those Filipinos know how to make a gal feel good. They booked the whole first-class section of an airplane just for Mama, Muffy, Peter, and me. When we arrived in Manila, there were eleven bodyguards waiting, our permanent escort. "Eleven bodyguards!" I marveled to Peter. "This is really the big time." Peter said: "Has it ever occurred to you that they feel we might actually need them?" At which point I grabbed Muffy and said, "You hold on to Mama's skirt and don't let go for the entire time we're here." The poor child was frightened half to death.

In addition to the bodyguards we had a large retinue—Mama and I were given our own hairdressers and private secretaries. The Filipinos have an interesting custom: if you admire something they are wearing, or anything in their homes, they will present it to you, usually right on the spot. It is a part of their natural generosity. Before we learned that custom we picked up quite a number of items! When I mentioned that I liked a particular fruit called a mangosteen that had been served on the plane, five hundred mangosteens were at our hotel door within a half-hour. When my husband admired a hand-embroidered shirt, he received twelve the next day. When I suggested to Mrs. Lopez that maybe I ought to have some gowns designed in Philippine fashion to wear for my concerts, she sent over her dress designer to make four beautiful beaded gowns for me—with shoes to match—and I was not permitted to pay for any of them. I admired a plate from the Ming Dynasty; I went home with it. My mother admired somebody's pearl ring; she went home with it. We had arrived in the Philippines with eight pieces of luggage; we left with seventeen, the additional nine pieces having been made to order for us.

At a dinner at the Presidential Palace given by the President and Mrs. Marcos, I decided to wear one of my Filipino gowns as an act of courtesy. Mrs. Marcos decided to wear one of her European gowns as an act of courtesy. Guess who looked prettier? Filipino styles are not meant to be worn by ladies as well endowed as I.

That entire stay in the Philippines was so luxurious, so surrounded by kindness that none of us will ever forget it. When it was time to leave, Muffy cried. Back in New York (we had moved there from Milton that summer) we were greeted by eighty-four cartons sitting on the white carpet in the middle of our empty apartment waiting to be unpacked. It was a hot August day and the air-conditioning was not working. I sat down on one of the cartons and cried and cried and cried, remembering all that luxury in the Philippines. The doorbell rang; it was my upstairs neighbor, Isaac Stern, with his fiddle. "Can I do something for you?" he asked. "Sit down with me on the carpet,"

I said, "and listen to me cry." We drank some wine together, I got over my doldrums and unpacked all those damned cartons. Peter, Muffy, and I had become New York apartment residents.

Not that I was ever there for any length of time. Early in 1970 I was invited to the Teatro San Carlo, in Naples. I was delighted: San Carlo has an even older tradition than La Scala and the opera would be *La Traviata,* with Alfredo Kraus singing Alfredo and Aldo Ceccato conducting.

Even the rehearsals were fun in the Neapolitan manner. The bass players were lined up against the back wall and Ceccato kept picking on one very fat one claiming that he wasn't playing neatly, not playing the right notes, and so on. This irritated the fat man no end: Italian musicians, the old saying goes, may not play all the notes right but they play the wrong notes with such heart. Finally the fat bass player could no longer stand Ceccato's criticism. He hoisted his enormous bass fiddle and stomped out, knocking down men, music stands, and music; it looked as though a tornado had swept through the orchestra pit. I burst out laughing. "What are *you* laughing at?" Ceccato asked me angrily. "I just feel sorry for him," I said. "Why couldn't he have played the flute, been skinny, and been nearer the door?"

Italians watch familiar operas like *Traviata* the way we watch soap operas: they know every word, every character, and they become as much a part of the performance as the singers themselves. After my second act plea, *"Amami, Alfredo,"* I left the stage as the audience applauded and went to my dressing room. It had been very hot and I was perspiring in rivulets. I took off the belt of my dress and my shoes and dabbed huge globs of white powder all over myself to try to dry off. Suddenly the door of my dressing room burst open and in rushed the head of the opera company. "Hurry, hurry, you've got to take a bow!" "What, already? Have Alfredo and Germont finished the *Di Provenza* scene?" "No, no, the audience is still applauding your 'Amami.' You've got to go out or they'll think you don't like them."

Taking bows *during* an act, stopping the action, is ridiculous. It will be the end of my career, I said, if I do. "Aha, Signora," he said, "*here* your career is just beginning!" So out I went, clutching my beltless dress, covered with great patches of white powder, and scrunching down so that the audience would not see that I was barefoot. Of course they saw and went wild. Next day the newspapers reported with a flourish: Before, I had owned La Scala, *now* I owned San Carlo. I am not usually a quoter of my own reviews but one in particular tickled me. "It took an American to teach us Italians how to sing *Traviata*."

Even the claque was a pleasant surprise. Its leader had come to visit me before the performance to make sure that I would remember his face and he had hovered around the opera house during rehearsals. But after the dress rehearsal, which was attended by the press as well as certain privileged citizens, he came to me and said, "Look, you're going to have such a big success I will just put on my dinner jacket and take some of my friends out for coffee after the performance." "Fine," I said, "my treat."

Lucia di Lammermoor had entered my repertoire at the City Opera in 1969 and in the next few years I found myself going mad all over the world —New York, London, Boston, Shreveport, Mexico City, Milan, San Francisco, Buenos Aires. It took me quite a while to work out my interpretation of Lucia. I went back to the original source, Sir Walter Scott's novel, *The Bride of Lammermoor*. As I play her now, she is not twenty-five, from a good family; she is more like a slightly older Juliet, vulnerable from the start, unaware of what is happening around her, a manic depressive entirely withdrawn from the real world. When we first began rehearsing the Mad Scene in New York, Tito Capobianco had a completely different idea from mine: he thought Lucia should exhibit more physical signs of madness— shakes, head rolling, and kicking feet. I tried it and fell to the floor, hysterical with laughter. So did Tito and that was the end of *that* version. It was Gigi Capobianco who made the suggestions to Tito for the Mad Scene in the successful City Opera production.

In Boston, Sarah Caldwell had ideas of her own for *Lucia*. In Sir Walter's novel Lucia stabs her husband thirty-eight times, so Sarah had my costume looking considerably more bloody than usual. For the Mad Scene she had built a ramp around the orchestra; she called it her "Hello, Dolly" ramp. Lucia's lucid moments were spent on the actual stage, but when she went mad she took to the ramp. It was a very effective production.

Opera, Rossini once said, is voice, voice, voice. He was wrong. Opera is music *and* drama. I'm prepared to sacrifice the beautiful note for the meaningful sound any time. Lucia, for example, has to sing a phrase, "This bloodless hand beckoned me into the well." What kind of noises, I wondered, would she be likely to hear from the specter? Normally it would be a wail with an embellishment. I took out the embellishment and substituted a chromatic scale, thus turning the sound into a short, not-very-musical wail. I did the same thing with Queen Elizabeth in *Devereux* when I felt the dramatic action called for her to shriek. I can make a pretty tone as well as anyone but there are times when the drama of a scene demands the opposite of a pretty sound. Take Tosca. In the first act she's consumed by jealousy; in the second act, by loathing. If the voice remains the same to portray both jealousy and loathing, then all the singer has done is let loose four thousand notes, got paid, and gone to bed.

I had opened the 1970 New York City Opera Season on February 19 with *Lucia di Lammermoor* and repeated it three days later. In the two nights between, I was in Boston singing *The Daughter of the Regiment* with Sarah Caldwell's company. It was a crazy marathon—commuting back and forth between New York and Boston, singing four performances in five nights of two different operas in two different cities. My Mad Scenes in Lucia were very, very realistic!

Poor Sarah! she was still looking for an opera house of her own. We performed *The Daughter of the Regiment* in the gymnasium of Tufts University. While we rehearsed, the track team was racing around the gym track doing its own rehearsing. The main dressing room was the women's locker room; mine was the men's locker room, and I made my entrance on stage through a back wall behind the basket on the basketball court.

Still, Sarah created another miracle. She turned the back wall of the gymnasium into a little village; all the locker-room doors became houses at different levels. Because there was no way of entering or exiting without being seen by the audience, Sarah used the audience as part of the action. People in the bleacher seats were given sheets of colored paper with instructions to please hold the sheets up when Miss Sills makes her final exit in the carriage up the center aisle. Everyone did so, right on cue, and all those sheets of paper added up to a most colorful French tricolor flag.

When I went to Milan to go mad again in *Lucia* later in 1970, it turned out to be the strangest engagement of my career. The *Lucia* that La Scala was doing was not a new production; it had been mounted the year before and was done with scrims, no scenery. The conductor, Maestro Nino Sanzogno, believed that every cadenza in the score La Scala was using had been written by Donizetti himself. Whenever I would sing a cadenza I had used somewhere else in the role, he would say, *Non è scritto cosi*, It's not written like that. If I asked to have a certain cut in the score restored, he would say, No, no, it is *tradizione* to make that cut. I have always found that when someone uses the word *tradizione* it means simply that about thirty years ago there was a singer who was unable to handle certain passages and so they were cut. And those sacrosanct cadenzas in the La Scala score, supposedly written by Donizetti himself, had actually been written, I learned later, by my teacher, Estelle Liebling, and had been brought to La Scala by Toti del Monte when she sang Lucia there. So much for *non è scritto cosi* and *tradizione*.

I did three performances of Lucia at La Scala—with three different tenors. Opening night, the tenor felt ill during the performance but finished up. I was not informed that he would be replaced the second night. When I walked on stage, going about my business, out came a dark-haired gentleman I had never seen before. He shook my hand on stage, introduced himself, and began singing. On the third night a new tenor emerged, wearing a red wig. He was so short that a good deal of his singing was aimed at my navel. On that night, too, I looked into the orchestra pit for the white-haired conductor of the first two performances; there instead was a bald head. No one had told me of the sudden switch in conductors—a dangerous move for *Lucia,* in which the conductor must be familiar with the singer's particular ornamentation and cues.

That whole experience at La Scala made me realize one thing: When La Scala puts on a special production (such as *The Siege of Corinth*), in which a great deal of care and love go into the selection of singers, conductor, stage designer, director, etc., they are unbeatable. When it does its regular repertory, however, it seems just an ordinary, rather provincial opera house, certainly not up to the overall quality of New York repertory opera. When I returned to New York, for my final Lucia of the season at the City Opera, it was like returning to paradise.

On April 15, 1970, at Philharmonic Hall in New York, I was asked to sing at a memorable occasion, the Salute to Pablo Casals, honoring his first visit to New York since 1964. During the first half of the program, while Rudolph Serkin was playing the piano and Leopold Stokowski conducting the orchestra, I sat next to Casals; his beautiful wife, Marta, had generously relinquished her seat so that I could chat with the Maestro. Suddenly I felt Casals patting me on the knee, then the thigh. "Look at that Stokowski," he said. "Look how young, how attractive, how strong he is." Then he smiled at me. "That's what happens," he said, "when you marry a young wife." I smiled back.

When Mr. Casals went on stage to conduct a piece he had written for one hundred cellos, Mr. Stokowski sat down next to me. Suddenly I felt *his* hand patting my knee, then my thigh. "Look at that marvelous Casals," Stokowski said to me. "So young, so strong, so virile. That's what happens when you marry a young wife." Stokowski, then eighty-eight, had married Gloria Vanderbilt in 1945 when he was sixty-three, she twenty, and the marriage lasted ten years. Casals was then ninety-three, his wife thirty-three; he had married her when she was twenty and he was eighty. I have often wondered whether those two incredible senior citizens had rehearsed the routine they did for me.

I was forty-one myself. What a late bloomer: that was the year I made

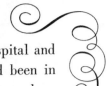

my debut in New York as a recitalist. Miss Liebling was in the hospital and terribly disappointed that she could not attend. Actually she had been in failing health and unable to teach for several years; I visited her whenever I could, and she knew and approved of the fact that I was working with Roland Gagnon, an excellent voice coach. She would insist on attending all my premières. Peter would pick her up in a chauffeured limousine, tuck her in with a woolen blanket, and get her to the theater on time. I remember one night when she came to hear me do Marguerite in *Faust*. She was then ninety-one. Next morning at seven o'clock my telephone rang. It was Miss Liebling. "Beverly," she said sternly, "that trill in the Jewel Song was very sloppy and slow. I expect you over here by ten o'clock." I had to agree—the trill *had* been sloppy and slow. Exhausted as I was that morning after the performance, I got dressed, went to her studio, spent forty-five minutes with her, trilling, and when I walked out I had a damned good trill.

At the end of my debut recital in New York I gave a little speech to the audience: how fortunate I was to have had only one singing teacher in my entire career, to have been with Miss Liebling for thirty-four years. I explained that she was ill and that as a get-well present I would sing a Portuguese folk song that she had arranged and given me as a birthday present when I was ten.

Miss Liebling died September 25 of that year, eight months after the debut recital. Ever since, I have ended all my recitals with a brief eulogy to her followed by the little Portuguese song, whose last verse goes:

> Tell me why you bid me leave you,
> There are tears in your eyes.
> Tell me why you wish our parting.
> Is not my love worth more than sighs?

She was a remarkable lady. I miss her a great deal. I miss her humor, I miss the funny luncheons we used to have. And I miss her calling me "My Bev."

A considerably more bloody than usual Lucia, I take my bows with the rest of the principals in Sarah Caldwell's production of Lucia di Lammermoor. *Sarah is the lady on my right.*

Muffy and me in our dressing room at the New York City Opera after our performances in Lucia in 1971. Muffy was making her debut as one of the candle bearers at my funeral in the final scene. When my "dead" body was being carried across the stage, my view of Muffy was blocked by one of the singers. "For God's sake," I hissed at him, "move your ass, I can't see my kid." He jumped and I was able to see Muffy. When that story was published, my mother phoned. "You didn't really say that, did you?" "Yes, I did." "I don't believe it," Mama said. "My baby doesn't use dirty words."

154

Luciano Pavarotti and I pour it on in a scene from Lucia *at the San Francisco Opera.*

On our trip to the Philippines Muffy and I shoot the "ra

Rehearsing with Miss Liebling in her apartment-s
not long before her death at ninety-one.

Opposite: Those two virile senior citizens, Pablo C
and Leopold Stokowski, at the Salute to Pablo Cas
concert in New York in April 1970.

14

Off on a Queen kick — a Bette Davis with high notes

As Queen Elizabeth I.

Queen Elizabeth I in Donizetti's *Roberto Devereux* first entered my consciousness as a possible role in 1965, when Tito Capobianco showed me a score of the opera. I was not familiar with it, and when Julius Rudel asked me after *Julius Caesar* to start thinking of what else I would like to do, Donizetti's Queen didn't cross my mind—I wanted to play Manon and Lucia too badly. But two years later, while on a trip to Europe, I found a score of *Devereux* in the Donizetti Museum in Bergamo, Italy, and on the plane home I read the libretto. At one point in it Queen Elizabeth says to Devereux, Earl of Essex: "It would have been better for you to incite the wrath of the gods than to incite the wrath of the descendant of the terrible Henry VIII." I got goosebumps and I said to Peter on the plane, "This is really a Bette Davis role with high notes. Now, if I could only find a tenor who looks like Errol Flynn!"

Julius Rudel had agreed that he would mount a new production of

Devereux for me. "By the way," he asked, "have you looked into any of the other Donizetti operas?" "Like what?" I asked. "Well, take a look at *Anna Bolena* and *Maria Stuarda*." "What are we going to do," I asked, "go on a queen kick?" Fateful words: that is exactly what we went on.

Roberto Devereux kicked off the trilogy of queens in October, 1970. The cast was phenomenal. Placido Domingo played Essex, and he did look like Errol Flynn; I played Bette Davis. Louis Quilico was Nottingham and Beverly Wolff was Sara. Julius conducted and the production team was the same as for those other memorable premières—*Julius Caesar, Le Coq d'Or, Lucia*—with the Capobiancos, Jose Varona doing my costumes, Ming Cho Lee the sets. All the ingredients were right.

My preparations for the role of Queen Elizabeth were enormous. I like to play characters who really lived because so much has been written about them. I read extensively about Elizabeth's life, about her physical appearance, from my own quite large collection of books on the Elizabethan period. She was a multifaceted lady and consequently, fascinating to play.

Gigi Capobianco created my makeup. She fashioned a bald pate made of latex to go over my own hair and painted my face chalk-white, slashed with heavy dark lines. The whole effect was remarkable, especially when lighting turned the black lines into the cracks and crevasses of an old woman's face. Because Elizabeth had been extremely vain about her hands and gesticulated with them a great deal, Gigi painted my hands with white paint, outlining the fingers in black to make them look slimmer. Originally I played the role with a putty nose—Gigi thought my own nose was too small for Elizabeth's—but when I perspired during the performance the nose would always fall off by the end of Act II, a most unregal sight. We decided instead to make my nose bigger with shadows.

My costumes were designed after paintings of Elizabeth in the National Portrait Gallery in London and in Woburn Abbey. The costume I wore in the second act weighed fifty-five pounds and was much too heavy to be lifted over my head, which already bore a wig and attached crown. Instead, the

159

costume would be spread out in the middle of a room, held upright by its own beaded weight; then I would step into it and two people would hoist it to my waist and hook it on. After the dress rehearsal my shoulders were covered with great bruises from the weight of the gown. My friend, Grace Miceli, of Grace Costumes, then devised a system of supporting strings inside to transfer the weight from my shoulders to my waist.

Converting me from Bubbles into Queen Elizabeth took more than two hours. In the years when I was playing both her and Manon in repertory I liked to point out that it took two and a half hours to make me up as Elizabeth in her sixties and only a half-hour to turn me into a seventeen-year-old Manon. Now it's the other way round: half-an-hour to make me a sixty-year-old, and two and a half hours to become a teenager. That's the way the cooky crumbles.

Tito Capobianco's staging was brilliant. Elizabeth's throne dominated the opera and he had designed it to be a haven for her. Whenever she felt threatened, whenever Essex was behaving in a displeasing way, she would retreat to her throne, heavily, an embittered old woman. The weight of my costume was a great help in getting the proper walk, and Gigi and I spent hours working on gestures. In one scene Elizabeth takes Essex's hand, points to the ring she has given him, and reminds him imperiously that the ring bears words spoken by kings. Elizabeth's attitude when she lifts Essex's hand and points to the ring with royal insignia, Gigi said, must convey to Essex Elizabeth's implied warning: Don't behave like a beggar. The key to the success of my characterization of Elizabeth lay in small touches of that kind.

There were times during performances of Elizabeth when I got completely carried away. In Act II, the Queen, in anger, slaps Essex's face. Gigi was always in my dressing room to remind me at the last minute that, before whacking Essex, I must make sure I switched rings from my right to my left hand; otherwise I would murder the tenor. One night she forgot to remind me and I forgot to remember. As I approached Essex to slap him, he noticed the big knuckle-bending rings still on my right hand—and he became the most frightened tenor who ever strode a stage. At the last minute, I remembered the rings and slapped him with my palm rather than the usual back-of-the-hand. He was so relieved that he claimed later he never felt the slap. Another tenor said that he was unable to hear a thing for two days after I had slapped *him*. And a third I once hit so hard that his mustache almost wound up as a third eyebrow. There were nights when Act II was so exciting that I completely forgot there was a tenor in front of me; I thought he was Errol Flynn and really wanted to let him have it.

The role of Elizabeth, I think, done properly, is the most taxing in the entire soprano *bel canto* repertoire. (Donizetti must have realized that too: although he keeps the Queen on stage throughout Act II, he at least provides scenes in other acts that do not involve her, so that she gets a chance to recuperate.) One cannot sing the role and come out of it unscarred vocally and emotionally. At least I cannot: I have lost as much as eight pounds during performances of Elizabeth.

They have been worth every pound. On opening night, when I came out for my bows at the end of Act II, the audience rose and applauded—the first time in my career that I had been given a standing ovation in the middle of an opera. I was very touched; no, more than that—I was ecstatic because I felt that the audience and I had just shared a marvelous experience.

Although Cleopatra in *Julius Caesar* was the turning point in my career, I think that Elizabeth is my finest accomplishment. I am proud of her, the first of my three Donizetti queens. To complete the trilogy—*Maria Stuarda* and *Anna Bolena*—would take another two years. But for now I was Queen Elizabeth and I hoped to continue to portray her to the end of my career. I really love that old lady.

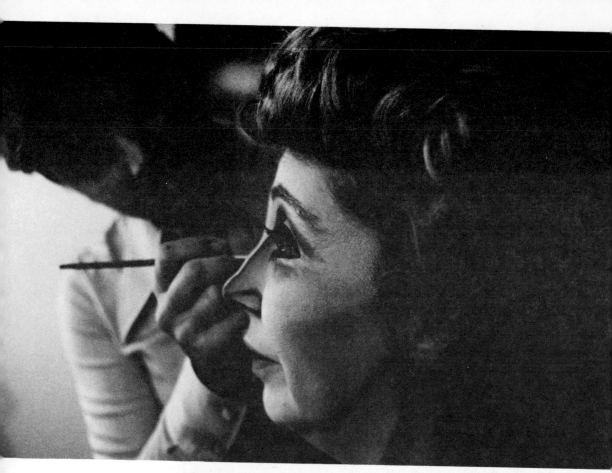

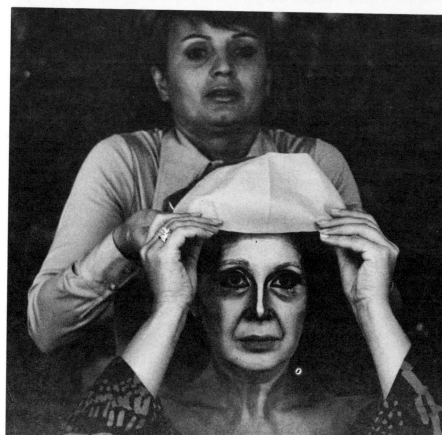

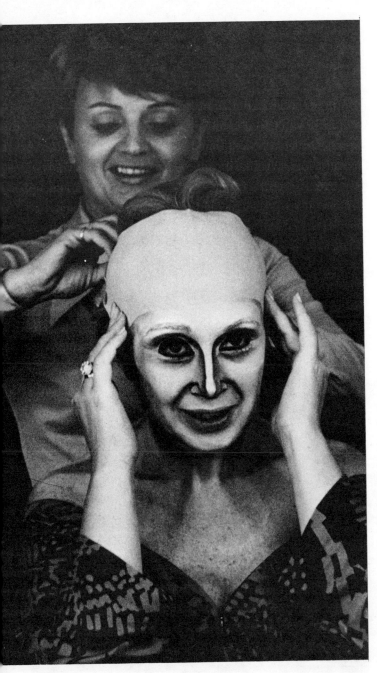

Gigi Capobianco goes to work to turn me into a sixty-year-old Queen of England. First she brushes in the black streaks to age my face (opposite, top), then carefully stretches a bald pate made of latex over my own hair (left and above). Add a wig, costume jewels, and crown and the transformation (right) from Beverly to Elizabeth Regina is complete.

Roberto Devereux, *Act II: Queen Elizabeth stands before her throne to denounce Devereux, Lord Essex (Placido Domingo, right foreground). In close-up above, Elizabeth is just about to whack Essex's face for his craven behavior.*

15

Nicolai Gedda and me in Manon.

*Moments when I deserve
to be where I am*

For a gal who had not sung outside the United States until 1967, I was certainly making up for it now. In January 1971 alone I sang three times in London, Berlin and Paris. I made my debut at London's Royal Opera at Covent Garden in *Lucia di Lammermoor* over the Christmas–New Year holidays of 1970. Three hundred twenty-four friends of the City Opera chartered a flight to attend that debut, and when the Mad Scene was over the stage was covered with congratulatory flowers. This antagonized some of the British press; they took great pleasure in referring to me as "Miss America, Superstar." But the British public liked me and the Covent Garden management was very solicitous.

With some reason: conditions for *prima donna*s were rather spartan, to put it mildly. The dressing rooms were small, the backstage chilly, and there was no heat in the bathroom, or the "loo" as the British call it. Birgit Nilsson, Margot Fonteyn, and I were alternating nights, and whenever I opened the closet of our common dressing room there, hanging up would be three simple woolen bathrobes; all that was needed to complete the picture was felt slippers. When you open your dressing room closet at the Met, say, or the New York State Theatre, it contains elaborate silky caftans in which you greet your fans after a performance. One night John Tooley, general administrator of Covent Garden, came backstage to inquire if there was anything they could do for me. "Yes," I said, "you can warm up the seat in the loo. It is the coldest thing I have ever put my backside on." He thought it was funny —I guess—but the seat never was warmed up.

Between performances of *Lucia* at Covent Garden, I flew to Berlin to sandwich in a *Traviata* at the Berlin Opera. Berlin was a very sad city. When I toured it with Egon Seefehlner, the head of the Berlin Opera (he is now head of the Vienna State Opera), he said, "You know, I'm probably the oldest thing in Berlin today." I understood what he meant: the city had been so destroyed during the war and then so rebuilt that everything in it seemed new. There was no stage director for my Berlin engagement; the management figured that this was just a revival, I was to do a *Gastspiel* and all I had to manage was my regular Violetta. Even Lorin Maazel, the conductor, felt at first that because we both knew the opera so well we needed no real rehearsing. "Let's have a good time," he said, "and see what happens."

As much as I admire spontaneity in a performance, I felt that we should have *some* rehearsal time, so we spent a delightful half-hour putting our *Traviata* together. It made me realize that "instant opera" exists in Europe, even in the important houses, as well as in the United States. Opera stars would be flown in on a few hours' notice to be plunked into a performance without preparation, without rehearsal. In our country, fortunately, that is now being done away with. Impressarios are demanding, and rightly so, that sufficient preparation time be allowed for their productions. Some are even fining artists for arriving late for rehearsals—up to $500 per day. That is a marvelous idea. I have always been a fanatic about showing up on time for rehearsals and I resent being kept waiting by late-comers.

On to Paris from Berlin for my debut there—an orchestral concert at the Salle Pleyel, conducted by John Pritchard, who was conducting my Lucias at Covent Garden. If I do say so myself, I tore Paris apart—audience, reviews, everything was *formidable*. It helped, of course, that I was very much at home with the language; I announced my encores in French. The French they are a funny race, but they do prefer people who can speak their language well.

Covent Garden, Berlin, Paris—they had all been satisfying, but my prevailing feeling had been that of homesickness. This was, after all, the holiday season, and even though my mother, Muffy, and Peter had come over for my London debut, it was not the same as spending the holidays at home. I made a promise to myself that never again would I be working away from home and family during the holiday season. Since then I have also made a promise to Peter never to sing in Europe again, because I don't want to be separated from my family for long periods. If I have any regrets about that decision, it is not being able to sing in Paris.

Shortly before that European tour, President Nixon had appointed me a member of the Council on the National Endowment for the Arts, and in February I was invited to sing at the White House. In the middle of the concert the zipper on my gown broke. Luckily Mrs. Nixon had suggested that I wear a dress with a matching cloak, because the room in the White House was rather drafty. When the zipper popped, I walked off to find the matching cloak to cover my gaposis. "My Walter Mitty dream," I apologized to the audience, "just popped in the form of a zipper on the back of my dress." Then I finished the program. The whole audience had seen the zipper popping and the talon flying. The papers, naturally, had a good time with it the next day.

Mr. Nixon was a solicitous host and I enjoyed Mrs. Nixon immensely. She invited me to bring my daughter Muffy for a private tour of the White House and Muffy and I did go back. Rather than disturb Mrs. Nixon, I phoned her secretary and asked her *not* to tell her that we were coming. But

just as we began our tour, Mrs. Nixon spotted us and insisted on being our tour guide. When it was over, Mrs. Nixon gave Muffy a piece of her daughter Tricia's wedding cake, all wrapped up. Muffy will never forget that day.

I have lost my temper on stage in public only once in my life—in San Francisco on April 30, 1971. I had been invited to sing a recital, not in the opera house but in the Masonic Auditorium. The acoustics were impossible: when I turned my head to the left, Charles Wadsworth, my accompanist, could not hear me, but I had to turn my head to the left because the sound of the piano bouncing off the right side of the auditorium was driving me crazy. Seats had been sold on stage for the concert, and in the middle of one of my Handel arias a little old lady had to go to the bathroom so off she went, down the stage stairs and out of the auditorium. I had prepared a very elaborate, difficult program. Six months' work shot to hell, I began thinking, and just popped my cork. I made a speech saying that it was the worst hall I had ever sung in and that I would never sing in it again. The press, of course, chastised me severely; *other* singers had appeared there and managed. Nevertheless, I have kept that promise. Neither singer nor public should be subjected to such atrocious conditions.

Up to that point in my career I had never sung Bellini's *Norma.* Then, in June of 1971, I gave my first performance of the role in Boston, in a production directed and conducted by Sarah Caldwell. I felt at the time, and still do, that Norma is not a very difficult role. The vocal range is not particularly high, the makeup is easy, the costumes light. Physically, then, it is not exhausting; as Birgit Nilsson would say, all you need is a comfortable pair of shoes. Indeed, I perform Norma in my sandals.

The production was a huge success. Sarah's theory was that one of the reasons the Druids had made Norma their priestess was that she looked different and behaved differently from the rest of them. She decided that I would play Norma as an albino, with a pure white wig. At her first entrance she was to go into a kind of trance.

I was quite concerned about that first entrance—how to convince the audience immediately that Norma was subject to epileptic seizures and different from the rest of the Druids in that way too. I practiced for days trying to get it right. One night after rehearsal I went back to the hotel, kicked Peter out of the bedroom, and practiced epileptic fits until two A.M. I must have done something right: at the rehearsal the next day the fit I threw was so convincing that several stagehands, thinking I was really ill, rushed over to help me stand up.

There are some lines in *Norma* that always make me want to giggle. Here is this woman who has betrayed her people by falling in love with the enemy, a Roman proconsul, and secretly having two children by him. At one point her lover, Pollione, turns to the chorus after Norma has confessed her treachery and sings, "Don't believe her, don't believe her." Norma sings back, "Norma never lies." That's one of my favorite lines. In another scene she tells Adalgisa, her rival for Pollione's affections, that she, Adalgisa, must take Norma's two children to Pollione and marry him. Well, what about you? the rival asks. Norma: You marry him and I will just kill myself. Instead of reacting in horror to the idea of Norma committing suicide, Adalgisa says, You want *me* to marry him? For me it is one of the classic funny moments in operatic drama.

I returned to London later that year to record *Maria Stuarda,* the second queen in Donizetti's trilogy. In the cast were Eileen Farrell, Louis Quilico, and Stewart Burrows—three singers with the same propensity for uninhibited laughter that I have. No recording session went by without some moment of hilarity. To sing with Eileen is one of the great joys of my life. We have exactly the same attitude toward singing: have a good time, otherwise stay home in bed. She had brought her daughter Kathy with her, I had brought Muffy, and we used to spend every singing and nonsinging hour together. My husband took his harem—Eileen, Kathy, Muffy, and me—all over London, wining and dining, and I have never enjoyed the city as much. Eileen's laugh and mine echoing through the restaurants and museums of London is still mind-boggling; we must have attracted a lot of attention. I wish that Eileen and I could find more projects to record.

Seventeen years after I made my first appearance with the San Francisco Opera, I returned to sing another opera—*Manon*, with Nicolai Gedda as Des Grieux. I was high with anticipation: to appear in an opera I considered my own in a production made to order for me by my director, Tito, and surrounded by all the glamorous brouhaha of a triumphant return— what a way to erase all those sad memories of my first visit in 1953! It *was* a beautiful *Manon*. In the San Sulpice Monastery scene, where Manon persuades Des Grieux to renounce the priesthood for her, a hush fell over the audience, that unique silence which occurs when people hardly dare breathe. When we finished the final *"Je t'aime"* duet, a roar went up unlike any I had ever heard before. Oh, perhaps at the end of an opera filled with blood and guts, but this was a quiet scene with just two people on a dimly lit stage. Nicolai and I ran off stage together, locked in embrace. My feet never touched the ground. Moments like these are what have made my career important to me. These are the moments when I return to my dressing room and say, "Okay, I deserve to be where I am."

Two scenes from my first Norma, *a Sarah Caldwell production of the Boston Opera Company in June 1971.*

With the Nixons at the White House in 1971—
scene of my zipper-popping incident.

My first concert—1971—with The Chamber
Music Society of Lincoln Center, which is headed
by my regular accompanist, Charles Wadsworth.
I don't know why Charlie is holding his head;
he says it's because of me.

174

My return—after seventeen years—to the San Francisco Opera Company to do Manon *with Nicolai Gedda as Des Grieux. I know that I will never sing* Manon *with a better tenor than Nicolai, and that's no mean compliment.*

*The hours
are long,
but there are
fringe benefits*

Getting stitched up in the Metropolitan Opera costume department for my debut as Pamira in The Siege of Corinth

Scenes from my Met debut, April 8, 1975. Harry Theyard (wh
plays my father), I as Pamira, and Justino Diaz as Maometto,
who wants to marry me, sing a trio at the end of Act I (above).
At left, Shirley Verrett, who plays the male role of Neocle wh
also wants to marry me, and I watch the rehearsal from off sta
The dress rehearsal (without wigs) of the scene in which I ag
to marry Maometto is at the top of the opposite page. And at
right, in actual performance, I'm singing my second-act aria.

Rehearsing the final scene of The Siege of Corinth. *Behind me on the right is director Sandro Sequi and the chorus.*

Upstaging my friend Bob Merrill in the Met lobby. When I was eleven and he twenty-one, in 1940, we sang on a radio program with the Morton Gould Orchestra.

Relaxing off-stage with some of the on-stage men in my life: Tenor Harry Theyard munches an apple and listens to me at the same time (above) during a rehearsal break at the Met. Top left, Norman Treigle and I dressed in our Julius Caesar *outfits backstage at the New York City Opera. Left, Justino Diaz and me in my dressing room during* The Siege of Corinth.

A typical off-stage pose—hunched on the bed in the master bedroom of our New York City apartment overlooking Central Park, phone at my ear, my five-year-calendar book at the ready for further entries. The tapestry on the wall is a Siamese one that Peter bought me.

◀ *The Greenough dolls, Beverly and Muffy, do their mechanical-doll number during a visit Muffy paid me at the City Opera during a performance of* The Tales of Hoffmann.

At home confronting my bedroom mirror:
"Mirror, mirror on the wall,
Is this my favorite role of all?"

16

"When will you stop this marathon?"

My father was a Romanian Jew who emigrated to this country with his family when he was a baby. My mother was a Russian Jew, born in Odessa. There she went to a school run by nuns, the only school in the village, and she likes to recall the many times that the nuns, who specialized in making and selling pickles, used to stuff her and the other Jewish girls into empty pickle barrels to protect them from marauding Cossacks. She came to the United States, via Yokohama, when she was fourteen.

In Brooklyn, we Silvermans were a typical middle-class American Jewish family. I had never considered myself anything but an American Jew, but, like most Jews, I had considerable curiosity about Israel. When I was invited to sing there in 1970 for the first time, with the Israeli Philharmonic Orchestra, my mother said, "Fine, but do the concerts for free. No nice Jewish girl takes any money out of Israel." The manager of the Philharmonic, Abe Cohen, was naturally delighted at the news that I would contribute my services. I was supposed to sing eight performances of a concert version of *The Abduction from the Seraglio*, with Julius Rudel guest conducting. While strolling through the streets of Tel Aviv, I kept noticing program posters announcing my concerts—my name in English, all the rest in Hebrew, which I cannot read. My name seemed to be showing up more times than eight. "Abe," I asked, "what's with all these concerts? I agreed to sing eight." "Don't worry about it," he said. "It's fourteen." "Fourteen! How come?" "Well," Abe replied, "the price was right."

Fourteen it was—I wound up singing every other day for a month. The Israelis had provided us with a chauffeur as well as a lovely guest house, and on my nonsinging days we all went sightseeing—Mama, Muffy, Peter, and I. It was Christmas–New Year's again, 1971; if we could not be in our own home at least we would be together. It turned out to be the best of all possible worlds. Our cast included a black tenor, George Shirley, a WASP soprano, Pat Wise, and an Armenian bass, Ara Berberian—a nice mixture of races, colors, and religions. The children got presents on Chanukah and on Christmas, and two holiday feasts with appropriate ethnic meals to match. They loved it.

One night Peter and I went to the Wailing Wall, the sacred wall in Jerusalem where men pray at one end, women at the other. Peter moved closer to the men's section of the wall to get a better view. I didn't know what to do—join the ladies or just stand there. It had begun to drizzle. Then I felt a tugging on the Spanish cape I was wearing. It was a tiny old lady. In a thick accent (I learned later she was a United States citizen who had settled in Tel Aviv) she said: "Nu? You're not going to pray? You've got nothing to pray for?" "Yeah," I said, "I've got something to pray for." "Then come, I'll show you a spot, you rub the spot, talk to God, and you'll walk away from the Wall laughing."

As we were walking to the women's section of the Wall, she stopped and looked at me again. I had no hat and Jews at prayer must have some sort of covering on their head. "Nu?" she said. "You've got nothing to cover your hair?" Then she dug into her shopping bag and pulled out a facial tissue about four inches square. "Here, cover your head with this." At the Wall she took my hand, placed it on a particular stone, and said, "Now rub, talk to God. You'll see, you'll walk away laughing." I rubbed the stone, said a few personal things to God, and suddenly I burst out laughing. There I was, standing in the rain with a piece of paper on my head, draped in a long black Spanish cape, wearing high boots, standing next to a four-foot-tall old lady, rubbing an ancient stone and talking to God. It *had* to be the funniest sight in the world and so I had to laugh. The little old lady looked up at me, in triumph. "See?" she said. "I told you you'd walk from here laughing."

I still consider myself an American Jew but now I feel a strong emotional tie with the Israelis. They are an incredibly brave people living in a wonderful country. While we were there we visited some of my father's relatives who had moved from Romania to Israel and that gave me a feeling of having roots there too. I made up my mind then that I would do everything I could to help Israel survive. And I told Peter—teasingly—that if he should ever convert to Judaism, it will have to be before the highest menorah in history.

After that Israel trip I returned to the United States to do some more *Norma*s and then, in Philadelphia with Luciano Pavarotti, my first *I Puritani*. I decided, before Luciano and I went on stage, that we had better straighten one thing out. I get intensely involved dramatically when I sing; Luciano has a glorious golden-toned tenor but is inclined to be somewhat less involved dramatically. He has been known on occasion, after an aria or a particularly successful duet, to bow and acknowledge the applause of the audience. In *I Puritani* the characters Luciano and I were to portray—Arthur and Elvira—are so difficult to make plausible to the audience that I felt any break in the flow or mood would be disastrous.

"Luciano," I said, "*no* bows during the acts. When we finish our Act III duet, that Philadelphia house is going to come down and the applause will go on and on. But NO bows." "Oh, Bevelina," he said, "one little bow doesn't hurt." "NO bows," I said. "*I'm* not going to break to bow, and if I see you start to break, I'll walk right in front of you and throw my arms around you."

The house, of course, did go nuts at the duet. Luciano and I were standing in a kind of semiembrace. He was looking at me pleadingly: A little bow, just a little bow. As he started to break, I threw my arms around him. He, not to be cheated out of his moment, pushed the sleeve of my gown off the shoulder, buried his head in my neck, and began nuzzling. He was having a good time nibbling at my neck, I was giggling because he was tickling me, and the audience ate it up. They applauded for fifteen minutes.

It is a joy working with Luciano. He is a big teddy bear of a tenor, always cheerful. He wears tiny French berets and enormous wide ties. On the road he always takes a hotel apartment with a kitchen; he loves to cook for parties, and if he invites you and four other people for dinner, he always has enough food for thirty and, sure enough, thirty show up. We did a *Lucia* later that year in San Francisco which the newspapers called "historic." But it is that first night of *I Puritani* in Philadelphia I will remember. Which of us won the battle I don't know, but we certainly knew each other better after that performance!

Maria Stuarda premièred at the New York City Opera on March 7, 1972. I now had two of my three Donizetti queens in repertoire. Of the three, Mary Stuart is easiest to sing—she appears in only half the opera, the first half being dominated by Elizabeth I—and I enjoy her the least. Donizetti did not portray her the way I feel Mary Stuart must have been. Unlike Elizabeth I and Anne Boleyn, she supposedly was a woman who ruled with her heart rather than her head. And yet Donizetti never wrote a single love scene for her; he makes Leicester more a friend and adviser than Mary's lover. As a result, you never feel that Mary is a truly passionate woman. Too bad, because John Stuart, who played Leicester in the City Opera production, is a very tall, handsome tenor.

Tito Capobianco staged the opera beautifully, especially Mary's death scene. I wore a red gown as I knelt at the chopping block. The masked executioner raised his sword, and as it swished down the stage went completely black. It was very effective: on opening night the audience gasped and one woman yelled out, "No, no!"

It was a relief to play Mary Stuart in my own hair and with my own face. It was also fun to portray Elizabeth one night and Mary a few nights later. In between, just to keep my sense of humor, I would fly to Shreveport or to San Antonio to bat out a fast *Daughter of the Regiment*. That same touring production of *Daughter* has played in more than fifteen cities and is always successful. The time has come: unless regional opera companies begin to share their productions, they are likely to go bankrupt. Opera companies should get together, agree on a single opera to do, and then have one stage designer prepare a production suitable for all their houses. It would save them all a fortune and opera would not be the expensive art form it is today, with every house trying to design its own production of the same operas. More and more companies in this country are beginning to work this way, starting with Houston and San Diego. It has worked with *The Daughter of the Regiment* and it has worked with Sarah Caldwell's production of *La Traviata*.

By now I was beginning to realize that I no longer enjoyed traveling so much, especially abroad. My life was turning into a rather lonely existence, the separations from my family longer and longer. Muffy, thirteen, was in school and even during summer vacations she didn't really want to travel with me; she preferred camp. My two stepdaughters were in college, leading their own lives. Even Peter was not particularly keen on following me around the world. He had his own interests, his own business projects, his own friends. He enjoyed going to Martha's Vineyard and urged me to agree to his buying land there and building a house. I felt it would be a waste of time and money—we would never be there enough. "Why not?" Peter would argue with me. "Why will we never be there? Why shouldn't we be there? When will you begin to slow down? When will you stop this marathon?"

The questions went unanswered, the property went unbought, and the marathon continued.

That year I was invited by the March of Dimes to become the National Chairman of the Mothers' March on Birth Defects. Theater people are always being asked to be honorary chairman of this or that; you're assured that it will not take your time or money, just your name on a letterhead. That approach, frankly, has always turned me off: if I cannot participate in an organization, giving either time or money, then why bother? Peter and I had long since decided that we would participate only in causes that directly concerned retarded or deaf children. When the March of Dimes approached me to help raise funds, to make speeches, and to talk to mothers with similar problems with children, I agreed.

Birth defects are very democratic: they strike everyone alike, irrespective of race, color, religion, and social or financial status. But *having* children with birth defects is a unique experience. Someone who has not shared that experience might put his arm around you and say, "Well, I know exactly how you feel." But he does not and he cannot. Only the parent of a child with a birth defect can talk nose-to-nose with a parent of a similarly afflicted child. I had never really talked much publicly before about my own children. It is the kind of situation in which you're damned if you do and damned if you don't. Some people think that if you talk about birth defects in your children you are trying to capitalize on their tragedy; others think that if you don't talk about your children you must be ashamed of them. I happen to be very proud of my children, and I felt that if by talking about them, I could help other parents in similar situations, then speaking out for the March of Dimes would definitely be worthwhile.

I also feel strongly that it is every child's birthright to be born healthy. We are so busy worrying about our future—men on the moon, solar energy, atomic energy—but our future is really our children and the simple truth is that we do not yet know how to guarantee a pregnant woman that her child will be born perfectly beautiful and beautifully perfect. If I could encourage

190

people to give more money so that children in the future would no longer be born with congenital defects, that too was worth my time.

The job with the March of Dimes has been one of the most rewarding in my life. I have visited child-care centers and hospitals where I saw scores of children with birth defects. I have talked with their mothers. I have met people whose lives are devoted to helping mothers produce healthy babies. As National Chairman of the Mothers' March on Birth Defects since 1972, I am proud and gratified that I have helped raise more than fifty million dollars. It has been as satisfying as anything I have done in my opera career.

Peter and me on our first trip to Israel, in 1970. We are standing in front of the huge menorah that dominates the landscape opposite the Knesset, Israel's parliament.

*On a Mike Douglas show in 1971, Burt Lancaster and I yak it up. I was co-host on the show.
Earlier, when I was in Los Angeles doing a* Manon, *Burt, a great opera lover,
came backstage and invited me to lunch. He wanted to make a movie of me as Manon.
"No way," I said, "I'll never let a camera close in on these wrinkles." "Don't be ridiculous,"
said Burt. "We could photograph you through gauze." "Gauze?" I replied, "You'd have to
photograph me through linoleum* before *I'd consent to make a movie!"*

At the JFK Center for the Performing Arts, in Washington, Tito Capobianco and I relax during the intermission of Handel's Ariodante, in September 1971. When Julius Rudel first proposed the unfamiliar opera to me, I suggested that we should call it Oreodante, since the two key roles were to be played by black singers and I felt like an Oreo cookie. The casting was changed: my lover in the opera was played by Tatiana Troyanos.

Two dramatic scenes from Maria Stuarda: *Mary
Stuart calls Queen Elizabeth a bastard. Whether that
confrontation ever took place is doubtful but it
certainly was an exciting moment histrionically.
Below, Mary Stuart's execution, beautifully staged
by Tito Capobianco. In front of me is the chopping
block. The executioner raises his sword, starts to
swing it down, and then—*BLACKOUT!

In April 1972, as National Chairman of the Mothers' March on Birth Defects for the March of Dimes, I visited that organization's Birth Defects Center at the University of Washington Medical School, in Seattle, Washington.

You ain't never sung with an exciting conductor unless you've sung with Zubin Mehta—as I'm doing here in November 1971 at a Celebrity Pops Concert in Los Angeles. That man can whip an orchestra—and a singer—into an unbelievable frenzy and he almost knocked me off the stage. We had the time of our lives, that moment when two artists meld into one.

17

God save the Queen—
with Duco cement

As Anne Boleyn in Donizetti's Anna Bolena.

*A*nna Bolena, my third and final Donizetti queen, went into the City
Opera's repertoire in the fall of 1973. It almost did not: the musicians were
on strike, and by the time the strike was settled we had exactly six days to
mount the production. Some critics have written that the opera is one of those
neglected masterpieces that deserves to be neglected. I don't agree. When I
play Anna, I bear in mind that she was the mother of Elizabeth I (who
appears briefly in the opera as a child). For me, Anna is like a high-strung
thoroughbred horse, skittish, independent and unpredictable. Not until the
final marvelous Mad Scene do I allow her to become soft and vulnerable. In
one scene I give Henry VIII a resounding whack in the face. During rehearsal
someone suggested that that was wrong, that Anna would never dare slap the
face of her sovereign for fear of being beheaded. Well, I replied, she *was*
beheaded, wasn't she? I won the right to slap the king. It may not have been
historically correct but it was certainly dramatically sound.

　　Bizarre things are always happening on stage during opera performances, but I think that one mishap during a performance of *Anna Bolena*

made some kind of history. As a result of an automobile accident in my teens, two of my side teeth had caps on them. One night as I was singing the two caps flew out. Henry VIII (Bob Hale) was just about to step on them (which would have meant the end of *my* performance, at least) when I grabbed the caps from beneath his heel. It was such a close thing that he skinned my knuckles. He, of course, was unaware of what had happened and when I pushed him back he could not understand why I had suddenly become so violent. Turning my back on the audience, I jammed the caps back on and finished the first act. During the intermission, Gigi Capobianco came up with Duco cement and we cemented the two caps in place. It worked fine. The only problem was that the next day the dentist had to use a hammer and chisel to remove them so that he could replace them properly.

Earlier that year my husband Peter had won his argument about Martha's Vineyard; we had bought some property and were building a summer home. One morning when I was in San Francisco to sing *Traviata*, the phone rang in the hotel. It was Peter: "Honey, something terrible has happened." My God, I thought, the children! Then Peter went on to report that our new house on Martha's Vineyard, which we were scheduled to move into in two days, had just been burned down by arsonists. I was so relieved, I began to giggle. It was only seven o'clock and I was still groggy. I knew that was not the reaction he was expecting so I said, "Listen, let me wash my face and brush my teeth and I'll call you back." When I did, I explained the giggle—the overwhelming relief I felt that the bad news was not the children but just the house. Houses, after all, can be rebuilt; we rebuilt ours in nine months—making all the same mistakes. But it is our dream house and we love it.

January 1974 was a typical month in a singer's life—at least this singer's. Recitals in Pittsburgh, Hartford, New Rochelle, Chicago, San Francisco, Denver, Columbus; three *Traviata*s in Houston; a benefit concert in Albany, New York, for the Lake George Opera Company; a couple of concerts with the Milwaukee Symphony. I was still a gal who couldn't say no; I could shake my head north-south with no trouble, but east-west was a problem.

We opened the New York City Opera Spring Season in February with the new production of *I Puritani* that we had premièred on tour in Los Angeles a month before. I have always maintained that opera productions do not have to cost hundreds of thousands of dollars; all they really need are imaginative directors and stage designers. We had them. Tito Capobianco came up with the idea for, and Carl Toms designed, three ramps that moved on a trolley carrying the assorted painted backdrops, and every time there was a scene change the audience applauded their ingenuity. Toms's costumes were also a vision. My own reviews were unqualified raves, almost as though I had written them myself.

It seems unbelievable to me now, considering all the *Traviata*s I had sung all over the world, that I had not sung a Violetta with the New York City Opera since 1963. Eleven years later I got another completely unscheduled chance. On March 20 the scheduled opera was to be *Medea* but the soprano who sings Medea was ill and Julius decided to substitute *La Traviata*. The only trouble with that decision was that Patricia Brooks, who usually sings Violetta, was off on another engagement. At one P.M. that day, Julius Rudel phoned: would I do it, just for him? He knew that I had sung two Anna Bolenas the week before and was due to sing *I Puritani* the next night. "Let me see if my curls are set," I replied. By three o'clock they were set and my costumes pressed; by five, I was in the opera house.

The 1974 City Opera production of *Traviata* had premièred the same year (1966) as *Julius Caesar* but I had never seen it. Only the first act was set in place, of course, when I arrived, and while I was familiarizing myself with it I told the kids in the chorus just to wing it. What a remarkable group they were: every bit of improvisation I did that night—about ninety-nine percent of the entire performance—they went right along with. When I picked up my skirts to do a can-can, even the boys joined in.

Julius was conducting, and although we had never done the opera together before, it was as though we had done it thirty times. I wore my own costumes (Patty Brooks's were much too small for me). They were a totally different period from those of the rest of the cast, but nobody seemed to mind, though at one point in the first act I was startled by a chorus girl dressed as

Georges Sand. It was, all in all, an "interesting" performance—nobody knew what was coming next. But I was delighted. And it was certainly better than having a dark night at the City Opera.

Rosina in Rossini's *The Barber of Seville* entered my repertoire that year in a Sarah Caldwell production in Boston. It was a typical Sarah production. Rosina wore bird feathers all over her costume to indicate that she was really a bird in a locked-up cage; Figaro, the barber, wore a red-and-white-striped costume and looked like a barber pole. A month before I went up to Boston for rehearsals, Sarah asked me to stop in at Rita Ford's antique music box shop on Madison Avenue and pick up a couple of mechanical birds in cages. "The birds," she said, "must have a good chirp and one that you, as Rosina, can imitate." "How will I know which one will please you?" I asked. "Audition them," she replied, "and when you find a couple you like, phone me and we'll listen to them on the telephone." So there I stood in Rita Ford's magnificent shop singing into the telephone to Sarah while the birds chirped away. We finally agreed on one. The production was such a success that after considerable urging from me, Julius Rudel agreed to bring it lock, stock and barrel, including Sarah as director and conductor, to the City Opera.

At all Silverman family functions, my mother used to trot out a favorite joke. "I'd like you to meet my two sons, the *doctors*," she would say, and then, introducing me, "and this is my daughter. Period." No more, Mama: that June at the Harvard College Commencement I, too, became a Doctor—of Music. It was a special thrill for me. The Greenough family had sent its sons to Harvard since the 1700s, and I had hoped to continue the tradition by sending my son there. When that turned out to be impossible, I kept the tradition going; I accepted my honorary degree not as Beverly Sills, but as Beverly Greenough. Mstislav Rostropovich, the Russian cellist, was given a degree at the same ceremony. We had never met before but I felt as though we had been friends for a hundred years. He is the dearest, huggiest man— we spent a lot of time that day at Harvard being huggy-kissy. When we were awarded our honorary degrees, the students gave us both standing ovations —it was a marvelous moment. I now have honorary degrees from Temple,

New York University, the New England Conservatory of Music, the California Institute of the Arts—and Harvard. That should be enough.

That fall season at the New York City Opera I sang *Lucia*, the entire queen trilogy—Bolena, Stuarda, and Devereux—and *I Puritani*. Looking back on that repertoire, even I don't know how I was able to do it. Still, I took on another new role, Donizetti's *Lucrezia Borgia*, in a new production in Dallas, Texas, mounted especially for me, with Tito Capobianco directing and Jose Carrera and Tatiana Troyanos in the cast. I never got to sing it then. While in Dallas, rehearsing, I got a call from my brother the gynecologist. Come back to New York right away, he ordered; those routine physical tests turned up a cancerous growth in the pelvic region that has to be removed. So I missed *Lucrezia*. But a fast healer, I was back on stage in three weeks, doing *The Daughter of the Regiment* in San Francisco and *I Puritani* in Los Angeles. I didn't want people to think I was dead!

In January of 1975 I was invited to sing at the White House at a State Dinner honoring the Prime Minister of Great Britain and his wife. President Ford introduced me in a most charming fashion. There is no more beautiful instrument, he said, than a well-trained human voice—and even though I was from Brooklyn, I had "made it." Danny Kaye, another old Brooklynite, who was also at the dinner, was so tickled that in the tape the White House sent me of the evening you can hear Danny whooping it up in the background.

Also in the audience, of course, were Mrs. Ford and Mrs. Happy Rockefeller, both of whom had recently undergone, as I had, highly publicized "female" operations. During the course of his introduction President Ford wanted to say that Beverly Sills was as equally at home in a Verdi ballad as a Strauss operetta. Instead, the words came out "Strauss operation." I guess it was the presence of the ladies. We all began giggling and he joined in; he is a great sport and a friendly man. Then he turned to me and said, "I'm not going to belabor this any longer." At which point he broke up, I broke up. "Mr. President," I said, "I'm going to see that you come along on all my tours to introduce me."

As Elvira in Bellini's I Puritani *at the New York City Opera, February 1974.*

At a playback session during the Angel/EMI recording of The Barber of Seville. *Standing at left is Sherrill Milnes. Seated next to me is Christopher Bishop, the producer of the album. The jolly curly-haired man is James Levine, the conductor, and at far right is tenor Nicolai Gedda. It looks like fun but actually I hate recording. On records a character gets built in pieces—not my way of working. I need to act and to use facial expressions, and I need an audience desperately so that I can communicate directly. I like to leave a performance emotionally* drained *and I never do after a recording session.*

Sarah Caldwell's Boston production of Rossini's The Barber of Seville in 1974 was a typically imaginative Caldwell success. The big bird in the big gilded cage is me, Rosina; the smaller bird I'm chirping to in the smaller gilded cage is a mechanical canary I auditioned for Sarah in New York City. She got the part. Below, the quartet is made up of Donald Gramm as Bartolo, Fred Teschler as Don Basilio, Alan Titus as a barber-poled Figaro, and Rosina.

As Anne Boleyn I tell Henry VIII (Bob Hale) off.

The Daughter of the Regiment *is an opera I've done for many years and in a variety of cities and productions. In 1970 I did a performance for Sarah Caldwell in a university gymnasium (above), with Spiro Malas as Sulpice, the sergeant of the French regiment of which I was the "daughter." Three years later I sang the same role of Maria in the San Diego Opera production. There I met my childhood idol, Lily Pons, for the first time. She came backstage (left) with the manager of the opera company and said to me in that marvelous French accent: "My dear, next time you must demand a white horse for your entrance. That's how I came onstage at the Met when I played the Daughter." When Miss Pons died a part of my childhood died with her. I'm so pleased that I finally got to meet her and that she turned out to be everything I thought she would be—friendly, talkative, and so French!*

Holding hands with President and Betty Ford at the White House in January 1975, when I sang there at a state dinner for Prime Minister Harold and Mrs. Wilson of Great Britain.

Like my brothers, Sydney and Stanley, I am now a Doctor—of Music. Harvard gave me an honorary degree at its June 1974 commencement. My citation reads: "Her joyous personality, glorious voice, and deep knowledge of music and drama bring delight to her audiences and distinction to her art." That's a long way from P.S. 91!

209

18

Sir Rudolf Bing and I—
"star-crossed lovers"

I meet the Met—1975.

On the night of April 8, 1975, I made my·debut at the Metropolitan Opera —twenty years after my debut at the New York City Opera, six years after La Scala, five years after Covent Garden. What, I am still asked, took you so long? In three words: Sir Rudolf Bing—who ran the Met from 1950 to 1972.

Mr. Bing had a thing about American singers, especially those who had not been trained abroad: he did not think very much of them as singers or of their ability to "draw" at his opera house. He made exceptions, of course, but only when he was in desperate need of a particular voice, usually a tenor or a baritone. One is never desperately in need of sopranos! I certainly do not blame Mr. Bing for not paying much attention to me in the fifties or early sixties—at that point not many other people were paying much attention to me either. But after my success in *Julius Caesar* in 1966, he could no longer claim that I could not sell tickets; all of my performances were sell-outs.

After my successes in *Julius Caesar* and at La Scala and Covent Garden, Mr. Bing came under increasing pressure from his Board of Trustees to find something for me to sing at the Met. He invited me to make my debut in *Lucia* and offered me the choice of three dates. The first, October 15, 1969, I was already scheduled to première *Roberto Devereux* at the City Opera. The second, December 24, 1969, I was scheduled to make my debut at Covent Garden. The third, January 8, 1970, I was scheduled to make my debut at the Berlin State Opera. It is common knowledge that opera dates are fixed long in advance; Mr. Bing must have known that I could not accept any of his suggested dates—even for the Met. I sympathize somewhat with Mr. Bing in his dealings with me. He used to say, "Not every singer can sing at the Met." I agree, but not every singer wants to—unless the role, the production, and the date are right, all of which I intended to insist on.

Mr. Bing and I were to have one other "misunderstanding." On the Dick Cavett TV talk show he made a few incredible statements about singers in general and Mr. Cavett invited me later on another program to answer back. Mr. Bing, seriously or otherwise, had said that singers are not really gifted, they simply have a disease: vocal cords. Most singers, he added, were uneducated and could barely read or write. My answer was that if you bought Mr. Bing's premise that talent is simply a kind of disease, it would mean that Isaac Stern, the violinist, has diseased fingers and Joe Namath a diseased throwing arm. As for singers being uneducated, I said that most singers *I* knew were educated enough to be able to sing in three or four different languages, and that they could read well enough to figure out the fee on their checks and write well enough to endorse them.

In an odd way, Mr. Bing made my career by keeping me out of the Met so long. Nothing infuriates the American public quite as much as the notion of a haughty, foreign-born aristocrat being mean to one of its native-born girls for some personal reason. And Mr. Bing had a part in my doing the Donizetti queen trilogy. Julius Rudel had originally planned for me a new production of *The Daughter of the Regiment*. That made Mr. Bing furious because he had already bought the Covent Garden production of the same opera for the Met. Julius and I decided that *Daughter* was not a vehicle worth fighting over. If it had been *Devereux* or *Lucia* at issue, I would have fought Bing to the death. Instead, Julius and I said, "To hell with it, let's find something more interesting." That's how those three Queens were born— and I wound up on the cover of *Time*.

In his book about his adventures as an opera impresario, *5,000 Nights at the Opera*, Mr. Bing mentions me only once. He describes how annoyed he was that the City Opera had scheduled my Donizetti trilogy at the same time as he was planning to produce it at the Met for Montserrat Caballé. "We finally accepted the fact," he writes, "that Beverly Sills of the City Opera, having been born in Brooklyn, was entitled to priority in the portrayal of British royalty." Enough said.

One day in 1973 in San Antonio, where I was singing *Traviata*, there was a knock on my dressing room door. It was the usher: Miss Sills, he said, Sir Rudolf Bing would like to come backstage after the performance. "By all means," I said. Sir Rudolf praised my performance and could not have been more charming. He was on tour publicizing his book and he had just made his debut in a nonsinging, nonspeaking role at the New York City Opera in an opera called *The Young Lord*, by Hans Werner Henze. "Mr. Bing," I said, "I understand you've just made your debut at the City Opera," "Yes indeed," he said, "and I had a lovely time." "Well," I said, "I always knew we'd both be working for the same opera company sometime." He had the good grace to laugh. The usher, who already had got Mr. Bing's autograph, then asked me for mine and I signed. "Young man," Mr. Bing said, "that's an historic document you have. It's the only piece of paper in the world bearing the signatures of both Rudolf Bing and Beverly Sills."

We met again in 1976, in the radio studios of WQXR in New York, where he was the host for a series of programs about opera singers. When he came to my apartment to discuss the program, we spent a delightful two hours talking. He has great wit and charm. On the radio I said to him, "Mr.

Bing, I feel that you and I are like star-crossed lovers—we came into each other's lives at the wrong time." I regret all the years that Mr. Bing and I were not friends; whether or not I sang at the Met was immaterial, but not being friends was a great loss to me. I'm so happy now that we've made up.

Sir Rudolf retired from the Metropolitan in the spring of 1972. One day early that year his successor, Göran Gentele, invited me to lunch. "Before we leave this restaurant," he said, "you are going to make me very happy and I am going to make you very happy." "I wonder," I said, "which will be the harder job." Mr. Gentele invited me to sing at the Met and he wanted me to make my debut in *I Puritani*. I told him that I would have to discuss it with Julius Rudel because I had already promised to do *I Puritani* for him. "How many years," Mr. Gentele asked me, "will you have to work for me before I get that kind of loyalty?" "It doesn't have anything to do with working," I replied, "it's because Julius has been my friend for twenty years." But at the end of the lunch Mr. Gentele and I were both happy: we had agreed that my debut would take place in 1975. That would be the first season that he would produce on his own. And I wanted to get the three Donizetti queens and other various City Opera projects out of the way first. I wanted my Metropolitan debut to be an isolated event.

Julius was reluctant to stand in the way of that debut, but at the same time plans for his own *Puritani* were advanced: he had an "angel" to pay for the new production and he had a tenor, Enrico di Giuseppe, who had the high Ds necessary. No problem, I said, Mr. Gentele will just have to spring for another lunch.

At that second lunch Mr. Gentele seemed vastly relieved when I broke the news to him. What he had not known at the time he offered me *Puritani* was that Joan Sutherland had been after Mr. Bing for years, with no success, to produce *Puritani* for her. If Mr. Gentele gave it to me first, it might create all sorts of problems later. It turned out for the best: I got my production of *I Puritani* at the City Opera in 1974, Joan got hers at the Met in 1976, and both were extremely successful.

It was my mentor, Edgar Vincent, who came up with the brilliant idea to make my debut vehicle *The Siege of Corinth*. Why not, he suggested, reunite Tom Schippers, Marilyn Horne, Justino Diaz, and me in the Benois production, have Sandro Sequi stage it, and show New York exactly what had set La Scala on its ear? That's just what we did—with Shirley Verrett replacing Marilyn Horne (she had decided not to do any more "pants" parts, our term for girls-playing-boys roles), and Harry Theyard, an American, replacing an Italian tenor. It was, once again, The Siege of the Americans.

The rest, as they say, is history. It is impossible to describe the tension, the excitement before my Metropolitan debut. I could not open a magazine or a newspaper without seeing my picture. I was welcomed at the Met like a long-lost child: everyone bent over backwards to be kind and accommodating. Schuyler Chapin, who had taken over the Met when Mr. Gentele was killed in an automobile accident in 1972, fulfilled every promise that Mr. Gentele had made me. During a break in one rehearsal, when Shirley Verrett, Justino Diaz and I were alone on stage, I muttered that I certainly hoped we could live up to all the hoopla that was being made over this. "How can we miss?" Justino said. "I'm a Puerto Rican, Shirley is black, and you're a Jew. We've cornered the market on minorities. Who would *dare* criticize us?"

Peter and I have always had a routine. When I leave home for the opera house to get ready for a performance, he always says, Have a good time. I reply, I'll probably sing like a pig. That opening night at the Met I found on my dressing room table when I arrived a gift from Peter—a little gold pig from Tiffany's, mounted on a chain. Outside the Metropolitan, Lincoln Plaza looked, my mother said, like St. Peter's Square on Easter Sunday. When I made my first entrance on stage to sing my opening line, *"Che mai sento?"* ("What do I hear?") I heard nothing but a tremendous roar from the audience. After my first aria the applause lasted so long that I got teary-eyed and had to walk upstage to compose myself. The curtain calls at the end of the opera were seemingly unending. Muffy, who couldn't hear any-thing, of course, but noticed all the people standing and clapping, kept

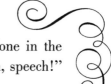

tugging at Peter: "Was Mama good? Was Mama good?" Someone in the audience let loose several screeching whistles and yelled, "Speech, speech!" It was my "claque" and fellow Brooklynite Danny Kaye.

I had already proved my revolutionary point: that one can become an international opera star *without* the Metropolitan. Nevertheless, I had grown up at a time when, if you wanted to see the really great baseball players you had to see Di Maggio and Gehrig at Yankee Stadium, and if you wanted to see an opera *star* you had to go to the Met. It is hard to shake that kind of indoctrination. Now, I had sung at the Met and I was the compleat opera star. On opening night the ladies and gentlemen of the chorus chipped in and bought me a gold charm bearing a replica of the Metropolitan Opera House. It made me cry—again.

My debut at the Metropolitan Opera:
as Pamira, with Justino Diaz as Maometto,
in a scene from Rossini's
The Siege of Corinth.

216

Sir Rudolf Bing and I—star-crossed lovers no more—at the studios of WQXR in New York
City, where he was the host for a series of programs about opera in 1976. Below, chatting with
Schuyler Chapin, head of the Met when I made my debut.

...king curtain calls after my Met debut, April 7, 1975.

The clan gathers at the Met. Peter and Mama, holding hands, chat with Joel Grey. Left, at the party after my Met debut the Silverman kids from Brooklyn whoop it up, brother Sydney on the left, brother Stanley on the right.

The champagne glasses are raised at my post-debut party.

19

So what do I do
for an encore?

Man plans, God laughs. I have always been a kind of fatalist. I firmly believe that what's going to happen to any of us is already written down in a great big book. Someone up there looked down one day, pointed a long finger at me, and said: "That one is going to be a singer with very high notes." I like that notion.

But if God gave me the pipes, I had to play them and it has not been easy. After my success as Cleopatra in 1966 at the New York City Opera, people began calling me an "overnight sensation." Overnight? God is laughing and so am I. There was never a straight line in my career, never a short cut. Some singers make it with ten roles; I had to learn a hundred. I never bought or slept my way into an opera role. If I was an overnight sensation, it was certainly the longest night's journey unto day that anyone has ever seen.

On May 26, 1977, I will be forty-eight years old and I have been singing since I was three. I have a repertoire of more than a hundred operas and I have sung fifty or sixty of them, in opera or concert form. I have sung in every major opera house in the world. I have sung with all the major symphony orchestras in this country and with many abroad. For the past five years I have averaged about a hundred performances a year. If not the highest-paid opera singer in the world, I am certainly among the top three. So what do I do for an encore? More.

I may slow down a bit—I say may!—but I have no intention of quitting yet; the five-year calendar book I always carry is booked through 1980. It is *not* the money—although there is certainly nothing wrong with making a lot of money out of one's talent. My husband Peter and I have always had an understanding: we would live on *his* money, and mine would be all mine to do what I liked with. All the money I earn now goes into a trust for Bucky and Muffy.

I still have many projects. I am bringing *Louise* back into the City Opera repertory this year and I'm considering more French opera. Julius Rudel has another Bellini work in mind for me in 1977. I'm planning an American première. And a world première: in San Diego in 1978, an opera based on a Jean Cocteau play. After I do *Thaïs* at the Metropolitan in January 1978, another new production is planned for me there in 1979.

And what happens when my voice finally gives out? I do *not* want to coach or teach singing: once I stop singing I intend to turn off all the voice knobs. But I would like at that point to help run an opera company; I know a good deal now about all the artistic phases involved.

It is very difficult to know when to quit. Peter says you quit when you can't do today what you did yesterday. I think it is much more subtle and complicated than that, more like watching yourself getting a new wrinkle every day and thinking that *this* is the last one until finally you shriek, "My God!" and say, "That's it. Enough." I have been in the public eye nearly all my life and it is not easy to give that up now. It's like hitting a home run and hearing all those cheers from the crowd—it gets in your blood. I have hit lots of home runs, and when the cheering stops I will certainly miss it.

Once a long time ago, when I was still growing up in Brooklyn, I came home from Manhattan very late at night. You must have had a marvelous time, my father said, you were out so late. No, I said, I had a miserable time; I had no money for a taxi and the subway took more than two hours. You mean, my father said, you sat there being miserable just because you didn't have taxi money? He gave me a twenty-dollar bill and said, Now you'll always have money enough to get out of doing what you don't want to do.

That's what I have now—the moral equivalent of a twenty-dollar bill. I no longer have to do anything professionally or personally that I don't want to do. And as long as I am having a good time, I don't intend to stop. Papa, who didn't live long enough to share my triumphs, would approve, I know. My mother says that she never goes to the theater alone: my father, she claims, is always seated next to her. We tease her that the woman actually sitting next to her must find it uncomfortable with a man sitting in her lap. But I agree with Mama: everything my brothers and I have accomplished *has* been witnessed by our father.

If Peter said to me tomorrow, Okay, that's it, I think I would be content to throw in the towel. (That may be easy for me to say because I know that he will never say it—he continues to leave my career decisions to me.) But I also know that when the time to stop has really come, my mother in her own quiet way, and Peter in his less quiet way, will let me know. Meanwhile, the fun is just beginning!

In January of 1976 Sarah Caldwell made her debut at the Metropolitan, the first woman conductor in the house's history. The production was La Traviata with me singing Violetta. Above, at dress rehearsal Sarah and I together in my dressing room. Below, tripping the light fantastic in one of the opera's party scenes.

At the annual San Francisco Opera fund-raising ball in 1973, Joel Grey, the master of ceremonies, and I do a tap-dance-soft-shoe routine. That was after we sang a duet from Mozart's Don Giovanni, "Là ci darem la mano." I told him he was the sexiest Don Giovanni I had ever danced with. He captioned this picture: "Bubbles and the Bantam." We've known each other only about five years, but from the first day we met—accidentally, in a museum with our children—we've been old friends.

Three days after my debut at the Metropolitan, I was back on the Met stage, this time with Danny Kaye in a show for children to introduce them to the world of opera. We too did a soft-shoe number and the kids loved it. Danny's rapport with children is second to nobody's.

With Johnny Carson on his TV talk show, 1974. He's Nelson Eddy, I'm Jeannette MacDonald and we're about to do our "Indian Love Call" number.

Carol Burnett and me doing song-and-dance routines in our Thanksgiving Day TV special, in 1976. When we were taping an eight-minute tap-dance number, Peter, who was in the audience, turned to my mother and said, "Hey, Ma, she's not doing so bad for forty-seven years old!" "Don't be silly." Mama replied. "She could do that when she was five years old."

The Greenoughs—alone at last! Muffy, now seventeen, is a junior at a regular private school for girls in New York City. She even speaks Latin!

I was Belle Silverman at three in Brookly
Now I'm Beverly Sills at forty-seven.
Plus ça change, plus c'est la même chose.

Credits

A great many of the photographs used in this book came from my personal albums. For permission to publish the others I gratefully acknowledge the photographers and organizations listed below.

Abresch, James: page 32, 47 right, 48
Angel Records: 204
Bagby, Beth: 125
Bergman, Beth (Copyright): 86 bottom, 105 bottom right and left, 108 bottom, 109, 116, 123 (all), 127 top, 129, 130 (all), 133, 134 left, top right, 154 bottom, 163 right, 174 bottom, 181 top left, 195 top, 198, 227 top
Birnbaum, Jesse (Copyright Time Inc.): 127 bottom
Boenzi, Olga, 218 top
Bruno of Hollywood, NYC: 21 bottom left, 60, 63 bottom left
Classic: 40
Drake, Fletcher: 194
Dunand, Frank/Metropolitan Opera Guild: 132, 134 bottom right
Fehl, Fred: 63 bottom right, 64 (all), 77 bottom, 80, 86 top, 96, 104, 105 top, 106 bottom, 115, 124, 164, 165, 195 bottom
Garrison Recording Company: 50, 56 (all)
Grossman, Henry: frontispiece, 135, 136, 157, 177, 178 bottom, 179 top, 180 (all), 181 top right and bottom, 182, 183, 184, 203, 206, 210, 216/217, 220 top, 221, 225 (both), 230, 231
Hagmann, Mark: 46, 76 top
Heffernan, James: 178 top, 179 bottom
Howard, Ken: 166, 175 bottom
Jones, Carolyn Mason: 226
Le Blang, Sedge: 77 top

March of Dimes: 196
Marcus, Helen (Copyright): 218 bottom
Marshall, Margaret: 107 bottom
Mazelis, V.: 76
McCombe, Leonard (Copyright Time Inc.): 156 bottom
McDowall, Roddy/Lee Gross: 158, 162 (both), 163 left
Meola, Eric: 131
Metropolitan Opera Guild: 132, 134 bottom right
Opera Company of Boston Inc.: 106 top, 107 top, 154 top
Opera Company of Boston Inc./Milton Feinberg: 205 (all), 207 top
Pan American World Airways: 79 bottom
Peres, Louis: 172, 173
Photo Emka Ltd.: 192
Pote, Louise: 89
Rebman Photo Service: 75 top, 87 bottom
Saxon, Reed: 197
Schwartz: 49
Seligman, Paul (Copyright): 219, 220 bottom
Seymour, Maurice: 22
Smith, H. S.: 21 top
Specht, Edward John: 207 bottom
Time Inc. (Copyright): 127 bottom, 156 bottom
UPI: 47 left, 63 top left
The White House: 174 top, 208
Whitestone Photo: 126
Reg Wilson/Angel Records: 204

Index

Page numbers in italics refer to photographs.